COME HOME

Tracing God's Promise
of Home Through Scripture

CAROLINE SAUNDERS

Lifeway Press®
Brentwood, Tennessee

Published by Lifeway Press® • © 2024 Caroline Saunders

No part of this book may be reproduced or transmitted in any form or by any means, electronic or mechanical, including photocopying and recording, or by any information storage or retrieval system, except as may be expressly permitted in writing by the publisher. Requests for permission should be addressed in writing to Lifeway Press; 200 Powell Place, Suite 100; Brentwood, TN 37027-7707.

ISBN: 978-1-4300-8533-1 • Item: 005846094
Dewey decimal classification: 640
Subject headings: HOME \ HEAVEN \ JESUS CHRIST

To order additional copies of this resource, write to Lifeway Resources Customer Service; 200 Powell Place, Suite 100; Brentwood, TN 37027-7707; order online at www.lifeway.com; fax 615.251.5933; phone toll free 800.458.2772; or email orderentry@lifeway.com.

Printed in the United States of America

Lifeway Women Bible Studies • Lifeway Resources
200 Powell Place, Suite 100 • Brentwood, TN 37027-7707

Cover design by Lauren Ervin

Editorial Team, Lifeway Women Bible Studies

Becky Loyd
Director, Lifeway Women

Tina Boesch
Manager

Chelsea Waack
Production Leader

Mike Wakefield
Content Editor

Tessa Morrell
Production Editor

Lauren Ervin
Art Director

Sarah Hobbs
Graphic Designer

CONTENTS

about the author

Caroline Saunders is a writer, Bible teacher, pastor's wife, and mother of three who believes in taking Jesus seriously and being un-serious about nearly everything else. She loves to serve at her church (it's not just the donuts), and every year, she retells the Bible's big story at a women's retreat that she and her friends offer local women through their parachurch ministry, Story & Soul. She's had the joy of publishing two Bible studies for teen girls (*Good News: How to Know the Gospel and Live It* and *Better Than Life: How to Study the Bible and Like It*), two picture books for kids ages 4-8 (*The Story of Water* and *The Story of Home*), and two retellings of selected books of the Bible for elementary readers (*Sound the Alarm* and *Remarkable*). Find her writing, resources, and ridiculousness at WriterCaroline.com and on Instagram @writercaroline. (And finally, let it be known that Caroline's kids said, "Mom can make a joke out of anything," and so she ran and added that to her bio.)

dedication

To the women of Story & Soul (especially my teammates and sisters Christin and Megan):

I wonder if you know how you have been home to me when I felt like I had nowhere to go? How I have tearfully praised God to watch as each December, the faces looking back at me grow to look more like family? Seeking God's Word on your behalf has been one of the greatest joys of my life. Thank you for enjoying His story with me. May this serve you.

WELCOME

In fall 2019, I committed to studying the theme of "home" in Scripture the following year. Of course, 2020 was, in many ways, all about home: we were trapped in our homes, we were separated from those who felt like home to us, and we became increasingly aware that this home didn't feel as safe as it once did. As disturbed as I was about the world, I marveled over all there was to uncover about home on the pages of the Bible. It starts with a perfect home and its tragic demise, contains story after story of people who aren't home yet, and offers God's promise to bring His children home. The more I studied, the more it became clear to me that "home" stretches far beyond a theological concept. It's deeply personal.

I began to catch the scent of heavenly homesickness on every person I encountered. In his song, "Not My Home" songwriter Luke Bower expresses this longing by stating "There's Eden in my bones."

Our lives have different shapes, and yet the longing for home takes up space in our hearts in a way that's both universal and seemingly impossible to describe. We all have our own ways to deal with this, like striving to make our current homes perfect or reaching back for old memories and happier times, hoping they hold the key to home.

But the Christ follower doesn't have to look around or look back to find home—she gets to look ahead. I wrote this study to root you in the truest story, to show you the Way (Jesus), and to help you walk by faith. After all, God has promised to bring His children home, and God always keeps His promises.

Caroline

HOW

to use this study

WELCOME!

We're so glad you've chosen to do this study! *Come Home* is a 7-session study in which Caroline Saunders follows the theme of home through the Bible. From humanity's first home to our eternal one, we'll see God drawing near to abide with us. We'll find that even the best aspects of home here are just a glimmer of what God is building for us through Christ. This study will affirm that our longing for home is good and purposeful, pointing us to our truest home which is found in Him.

GETTING STARTED

Because we believe discipleship happens best in community, we encourage you to do this study together in a group setting. Or, if you're doing this alone, consider enlisting a friend or two to go through it at the same time. This will give you study friends to pray with and connect with over coffee or through text or email so you can chat about what you're learning.

Here's a look at what you can expect to find in this study.

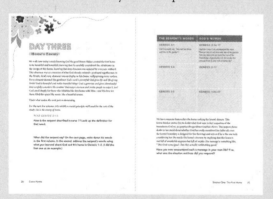

PERSONAL STUDY

Each week features five days of personal study to help you trace the theme of home through Scripture. You'll find questions to help you understand and apply the text, plus insightful commentary to clarify your study.

To access the video teaching sessions, use the instructions in the back of your Bible study book.

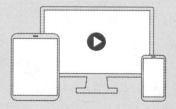

LETTERS

Day 5 of each week features a letter that expresses the writer's personal experience with home. The authors of these letters are women from different walks of life. You'll have space to share how each letter resonated with you and helped you understand God's view of home.

POEMS

Caroline closes every video teaching with a poem that captures the heart of that message. We've included them in written form at the end of each session for you to reflect on.

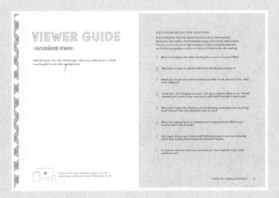

VIEWER GUIDE

At the beginning of each session, you'll find a video viewer guide. These pages provide space for you to take notes during the video teaching and questions to help you internalize and apply what you've heard. If you're studying with a group, these pages will drive your video teaching discussion. If you're doing this study solo, use this space as a reflection time.

LEADING A GROUP?

A free leader guide PDF is available for download at **lifeway.com/comehome**. The leader guide offers several tips and helps along with discussion guides for each week. At that website you'll also find free downloadable resources to help you promote the study in your church or neighborhood, including: an invitation card, promotional poster, bulletin insert, and PowerPoint® template.

the

first

home

session one

It was very good indeed.

GENESIS 1:31b

Home is a rich word, isn't it? It's hard to define, yet universally understood. We know when we miss it, we remember times we've experienced a measure of it, and we always find ourselves trying to get to it. Ingrained but elusive. Perhaps this is why we're so prone to look back—to try and grasp again what we once had. However, when we look at God's story of home in the Bible, it's clear that for the Christ follower, home is not behind. Home is ahead. We're all spiritually homesick, thinking we're longing for something we once had, while actually longing for something we've yet to have, something promised to God's people.

In this week's study, we're going to look at the first home. God made it, and it was wonderful. But this perfect home was lost, and homesickness pinched within the first human hearts. Yes, there's an enemy of home against which we all need to stand guard, but God promised to defeat this enemy and make the way home.

VIEWER GUIDE

session one

Watch the Session One video. Use this page to take notes, capture quotes, or doodle some thoughts from the video teaching session.

To access the video teaching sessions, use the instructions in the back of your Bible study book.

DISCUSSION/REFLECTION QUESTIONS

If you're doing this study with a group, be ready to discuss these questions during your time together. (If you're leading a group, check out the leader guide at **lifeway.com/comehome** to help you prepare.) If you're doing this study solo, use the following questions to reflect on what you've heard in the video teaching.

1   What is one thing in the video teaching that stood out to you? Why?

2   How would you finish this statement "To me, home is . . . "?

3   What does the goodness and abundance of the first home teach us about God? Does that challenge your thoughts on God in any way? Explain.

4   In what areas of your life do you currently see God's goodness on display?

5   Generally speaking, how have you seen sin wreak havoc on homes around you?

6   How does Satan tempt you to doubt God? How does he tempt you to be suspicious of God's life-giving boundaries?

7   How do you see God speak and act redemptively in the closing part of this story? How does that give you hope in your struggles with sin?

8   If someone asked you what you learned in our time together today, what would you say?

DAY ONE

The Good Home Maker

No one makes a home like God.

> *LOOK UP PROVERBS 3:19 AND HEBREWS 11:3* **and write both verses below.**

How do these verses enhance your understanding of the creation narrative?

God built the first home with His word—with His wisdom! (Find a contractor who can do that.) The first home was spectacularly lovely and jam-packed with the fruit of God's wisdom, crammed with evidence that God's word is powerful.

DAY 1 OF CREATION INTRODUCES US TO A PATTERN: GOD *SAYS*, GOD *SETS*, GOD *SHOWS*.

- God **said**, "Let there be light," and then, BOOM! there was light.

- He also **set** a life-giving boundary—sometimes the light would light (day), and sometimes the light would not (night).

- God **showed** His goodness. God called the light good, and of course it was.

Let's pay attention to Genesis 1:6-25, keeping an eye out for the *says, sets, shows* pattern. If you're comfortable writing in your Bible, you can label these things as you read the passage. (For example, you could underline the words God *said*, circle the boundary God *set*, and star the goodness God *showed*.)

Promise me you won't overthink this, okay? Feel at home in the pages of God's Word, and don't worry too much about mistakes.

If you're hesitant to scribble in your Bible or simply like to fill out a worksheet, you are also free to record what you notice on these pages. As you read, you may want to place a question mark by anything that confuses you.

Maybe a future study day will answer your question, or perhaps you can discuss it with your group when you meet.

I'm telling you, do not overthink this. That mean teacher from high school will not be grading your work.

DAY 2: GENESIS 1:6-8

What did God *say*?

What boundary did God *set*?

How did God *show* His goodness?

DAY 3: GENESIS 1:9-13

What did God *say*?

What boundary did God *set*?

How did God *show* His goodness?

DAY 4: GENESIS 1:14-19

Note: Here God set up the rhythms that form our lives—seasons, days, and years. Notice that He made it so much more than a calendar. He made it beautiful! How many of us have tried to take a picture of a sunset or a starry sky and discovered no camera could truly capture it?

What did God *say*?

What boundary did God *set*?

How did God *show* His goodness?

DAY 5: GENESIS 1:20-23

What did God *say*?

What boundary did God *set*?

How did God *show* His goodness?

DAY 6, BEFORE MAN: GENESIS 1:24-25

What did God *say*?

What boundary did God *set*?

How did God *show* His goodness?

When you've finished paying attention to Genesis 1:6-25, check this box ☐.
(There's no reason for this except that we just love a box-checking moment.)

As you noted, this *says, sets, shows* pattern holds from days two through six of creation. Sometimes God shows His goodness in an obvious way ("God saw that it was good" is a common refrain), and sometimes the goodness is implied by the beauty and bounty of His creation. This is a really wonderful thing to consider about God: He didn't have to make things wonderful, but He did!

How does this description of God compare with your current view of Him?

Confession: I'm prone to think of God as a grumpy, cross-armed principal with a weird mustache, bad suit, coffee breath, and clipboard where He records my many indiscretions. He might say, "Late again, I see," or "Well, I'll forgive you, but I'm not happy about it" or rattle off a bunch of rules designed to squash any semblance of fun. The creation narrative (and probably every other part of the Bible) blows my wrong view of God to smithereens. As we read about our Creator God shaping this beautiful, bountiful home, it's clear His word is powerful, His boundaries are life-giving, and His goodness is evidenced everywhere. God is not a cross-armed authoritarian whose office we want to avoid or slink away from, but an open-armed Home Maker whose home we want to run to!

Let's reflect.

This narrative is full of life! God offers life-giving words, God offers life-giving boundaries, and God gives His creation the ability to create more life. How does this shape how you view God?

1. What does this creation narrative reveal about God's words?

2. How can the creation narrative inform how you view God's boundaries?

3. How does the creation narrative strengthen you to remember God's goodness?

4. Think about the pattern: the words God *says*, the boundaries God *sets*, and the goodness God *shows*. How might these elements impact how you understand home? How you understand God?

5. Is there any part of today's text that you'd like to talk over with another believer? Write his or her name below, and make a plan to reach out to that person this week.

Too often, we're tempted to be like Eve and think God is holding out on us (Gen. 3:1-7). But the Eden narrative resets our wonky inner compass. God is not just good—He's the author of good! God not only gives us our lives—He makes our lives lively! The first home equips us to wipe the smudge off our glasses and view the whole concept of home through a clearer lens. Truly, we can trust God's promises of home—because the whole notion of home has its origin in Him alone.

DAY TWO

The Together Home

We've all been in beautiful, bountiful homes—homes that look great and have great stuff—yet don't seem homey. We get the feeling that such homes aren't for living and that such homes don't have us in mind. We're too prone to spill stuff. We'll push the wrong button on the remotes and accidentally destroy the carefully designed settings of technology we don't understand. We are too human for such homes.

But here's wonderful news: God made the first home *with humanity in mind!* Consideration and closeness are woven into the fabric of the creation story. God made a home where humans could be with Him, and it was every bit as wonderful as you can imagine.

> *LOOK UP THE FOLLOWING VERSES.* **How does each one help you understand God's purpose for creation?**
>
> **Psalm 115:16**
>
>
>
> **Isaiah 45:18**

This narrative is about to go "grape juice on the white carpet," but before it does, let's once again soak in the goodness of this first home.

> *REVIEW GENESIS 1 AND READ GENESIS 2* **with two specific themes (repeated ideas) in mind: consideration and closeness.**

- God's *consideration* for humanity—How does the text reveal God's hospitality? In other words, how can you tell that God thoughtfully shaped this home in anticipation of those who would share it with Him?

- The *closeness* that was enjoyed in this home—What details point to togetherness?

NOW, LOOK UP THE FOLLOWING VERSES FROM THOSE CHAPTERS **and note how each one reveals one of those themes.**

Genesis 2:8-9

Genesis 2:16-17

Genesis 2:18

Genesis 2:23

Genesis 2:25

God created this home not just for Himself and not just for humanity. God created this home for humanity to be *with* Him. (Pause for effect. This truth really ministers to me.)

Think about what you already know about God and the Bible (whether it's a lot or a little). What evidence is found in Scripture of God's desire to be *with* people?

One thing we need to be clear about: before this first home, God wasn't sitting around, twiddling His holy thumbs and wishing He had someone to hang out with. Remember this truth about the Trinity: God is one, and yet God is three. God the Father, God the Son, and God the Spirit are one, yet because God is three persons, God enjoys perfect closeness and community. Like we talked about in this session's teaching time, the first home is not the *invention* of togetherness but the *extension* of it. The inhabitants of the first home were invited to experience what God Himself already enjoys: togetherness.

What images, memories, or ideas come to your mind when you hear the word *togetherness*?

Based on your life experiences, why does togetherness matter?

Based on the creation narrative, why does togetherness matter?

Here's something interesting from behind the scenes of the formation of this Bible study: as we brainstormed the title, we realized it is impossible to find an appropriate synonym for the word "home." If you go hunting for synonyms, you'll find a bunch of words that fall short, like "dwelling," "abode," "house," "apartment." After every single one was mentioned, we said, "Ew, no, that's not it!" None of those words work. They're just place words, structure words—and there's something in us that innately understands that home isn't simply a place or a structure. Home is people, too. And really, home isn't merely people—it's about the closeness people share and the consideration they have for one another. Even when we live alone, we understand the treasure of inviting others over for dinner or experiencing the hospitality of others! Home is a togetherness word, and something like "dwelling" falls terribly short.

How would you define "home"? *(If you find it hard to define, consider listing some home moments you've experienced. That'll cut to the heart of the meaning better than a dictionary-like definition.)*

Jean Val Jean didn't sing, "Bring him to the dwelling" in *Les Miserables* (and if he did, none of us would snot-cry the way we do when he sings "Bring Him Home"). Michael Buble's 2005 song "Home" wouldn't have worked with the word "abode," and John Denver couldn't have crooned, "Take me to my lodging, country roads." Without the word *home*, these emotion-packed lyrics suddenly sound like they were written by robots.

I think the reason these supposed synonyms won't work in place of *home* is because they all lack the idea of togetherness. Home is supposed to be a together place; it always has been. It was that way from the beginning by God's design. Our longing to be considered in our homes, our longing to be close to God and others in our homes—it all makes sense, doesn't it?

LOOK UP GENESIS 3:8 **and write it below.**

This verse occurs after sin entered the picture, but it also gives us a glimpse of what garden of Eden togetherness might've been like. God was walking in the cool of the day; the man and woman heard Him.

That day, Adam and Eve hid. But it's clear that hadn't always been the case. The Hebrew word for God's action in this verse indicates this was a habitual practice.[1] How many moments of *not hiding* did Adam and Eve enjoy before sin intruded their hearts, unpacking its suitcase of shame and separation? We can't know. Even still, in our hearts, we long for this garden togetherness.

Has this part of God's story of home stirred up any longings in your heart? Tell me about it. *(Pssst. It's okay if the answer is no.)*

Is there any part of today's text that you'd like to talk over with another believer? If so, write his or her name below, and think about reaching out to that person.

DAY THREE

Home's Enemy

We walk into today's study knowing God the good Home Maker created the first home to be beautiful and bountiful, knowing that He carefully considered the inhabitants in the design of this home, knowing that deep closeness was enjoyed by everyone within it. This closeness was an extension of what God already enjoyed—profound togetherness in the Trinity. God's very character was on display in this home, wallpapering every surface. Every element shouted His goodness: *God's word is powerful! God gives life and life-giving limits! God is beautiful and makes beautiful things! God is generous and gives abundantly! God carefully considers His creation! God enjoys closeness and invites people to enjoy it, too!* God cared deeply for those who inhabited the first home with Him—and His love for them filled the space like music, like a beautiful aroma.

That's what makes the next part so devastating.

For the next few minutes, let's solidify a crucial principle we'll need for the rest of the study: *Sin is the enemy of home.*

READ GENESIS 3:1-5.

How is the serpent described in verse 1? Look up the definition for that word.

What did the serpent say? On the next page, write down his words in the first column. In the second, address the serpent's words using what you learned about God and this home in Genesis 1–2. (I did the first one as an example.)

THE SERPENT'S WORDS	GOD'S WORDS
GENESIS 3:1 Did God really say, "You can't eat from any tree in the garden"?	**GENESIS 2:16-17** And the LORD God commanded the man, "You are free to eat from any tree of the garden, but you must not eat from the tree of the knowledge of good and evil, for on the day you eat from it, you will certainly die."
GENESIS 3:4	**GENESIS 2:17**
GENESIS 3:5	**GENESIS 1:26-27**

We have someone from within the home seeking the home's demise. This home-breaker invites Eve to doubt what God *says*; to feel suspicious of the boundaries God *set*; to question the goodness God has *shown*. The serpent places doubt in her mind about whether God has really *considered* her (after all, even the home's boundary is designed for her thriving) and acts as if he is the one truly considering her. He attacks the home's *closeness* by implying that this home is not full of wonderful surprises but full of secrets. His message is something like, "This God seems good—but He's actually withholding good."

Have you ever encountered such a message in your own life? If so, what was the situation and how did you respond?

God's word plays a powerful role in the formation of the first home. What role does *disbelieving* God's word play in the corruption of the first home?

This serpent is a bold dude. Imagine speaking deceptively about God in His house! Imagine questioning the words of the One who created all things with His words! The serpent has come to undermine the home's very foundation.

LET'S LOOK AT GENESIS 3:6-13.

In verse 6, Eve admires three qualities about the fruit. *LOOK UP GENESIS 2:9.* **How does this verse affirm that the first two qualities Eve admires are actually true?**

The third quality—the tree's ability to make one wise—is beyond its scope. According to Proverbs 9:10, what's the actual source of wisdom?

Proverbs 3:19 says, "The Lord founded the earth by wisdom." Mankind was literally surrounded by the fruit of God's wisdom—yet they looked to a forbidden tree for wisdom rather than to the God who made it.

Nancy Guthrie says that here, at the tree of the knowledge of good and evil, "Adam was meant to judge good as good and evil as evil according to what God had said. It was there that Adam should have crushed the head of the serpent when he tempted Eve to eat of this tree. But he didn't."[2]

Adam and Eve were told their eyes would be uncovered (Gen. 3:5), but they didn't understand that this uncovering would be violating. It wasn't the soft glow of a lamp but the searing brightness of a spotlight. In trying to see like God, they ironically blinded themselves, and a veil descended upon human hearts that would not lift until Calvary. *(Aren't you excited to experience the unfolding of this story?)*

What do Adam and Eve do in verse 7 to address their shame? Do you think this actually helped?

Have you ever responded to your sin and shame in a similar fashion? Explain.

In Genesis 2:25, man and woman were described as "naked, yet felt no shame," but now, after sin, they frantically sought to cover themselves. Even though we've always lived in a sinful world, this instinct isn't difficult for us to understand. I mean, being naked in your own home or in front of a trusted spouse isn't really a big deal and is even an indication of comfort or intimacy. But being naked in a place that is not home or in front of a stranger? Well, that's the stuff of nightmares. (We have all had this very nightmare.) Clearly, home had shifted. Everything had shifted.

Where in Genesis 3:6-13 do you see the following results of sin?

Shame

Exposure

Hiding

Blame

Sin makes big promises of life, but it only brings death. Adam and Eve's physical home wasn't destroyed, yet everything that made home feel like home was destroyed through sin's deception. Adam and Eve's physical bodies didn't immediately drop dead, but the process of death had begun. Plus, spiritual death took place with their separation from God. Their relationship was broken. And their sin caused the venom of sin to begin to seep into the world's veins.

They hungered for glory, but they found shame. They had been living in a home where they were considered and seen, but now they'd been tricked and exposed. They wanted to be outside of God's design, so they took the step to do so, thinking it would be life—only to realize it was death.

The creation narrative reminds us that home is God's design and anything outside of God's design is sin. It also warns us: If we are to be people who cling to God's promises of home, we have to clearly understand that sin is the enemy of home.

Let me restate something from the teaching video that's foundational for our understanding of God's story of home. Throughout this study, you'll hear me say that sin is the *enemy of home*. It is. Pride, jealousy, selfishness, rage, immorality, and other sin rips at the fabric of our earthly homes. But know that behind sin is an *enemy of God*: the serpent (also known as Satan, the devil, the deceiver, the accuser, etc.). He was the one who introduced sin into the first home, and he still works to tempt us to sin. We must be on guard against sin, always ready to recognize it as an enemy, as something that will bring death.

Adam and Eve are often called "our first parents," and we've inherited a lot from them. Like them, our hearts are desperate to be like God in ways He did not design. Our ears, too, are attuned to Satan's lies and numbed to God's truth. Though many of our personal stories of home are punctuated with glimmers of Eden found in Genesis 1–2, all of our stories are shadowed with the darkness of Genesis 3. Our personal sin, the sin of others, and the generational impact of sin intrude upon our places, our people, and our peace. Because sin has been reigning since the days of Adam and Eve, all of us endure homes that are broken on some level. All of us are homesick.

How has the enemy of sin affected your story of home?

Take heart, sister: Sin is a true enemy, and yet, in the story of the Bible and in our own stories, sin does not have the final word. Tomorrow we'll look into how God addresses this enemy.

DAY FOUR

Home Lost

Sin is the enemy of home, but here is some good news: God will always, always deal with this enemy. God is not just a Home Maker; He is a Home Defender.

How did God deal with this first sin? He punished it through a series of curses—first the serpent, then the woman, then the man.

THE SERPENT – GENESIS 3:14-15

Notice that the curse to the serpent contains a promise for humanity.

Write verse 15 below and highlight it in your Bible.

This is God's first promise of home! One day, the offspring of a woman would strike the sin-promoting serpent's (Satan) head—dealing him an eternally deadly blow and eliminating sin's power. But this defeat of the enemy would be costly, because the offspring of woman, Jesus, would be struck, too. But through Jesus's death and subsequent resurrection, God would provide humanity a grace-lined path home.

THE WOMAN AND THE MAN – GENESIS 3:16-19

Next up came curses for Eve and then Adam. Notice that the curses are simultaneously an act of judgment and a pronouncement of natural consequence. Adam and Eve wanted to step outside of God's design to reach for their own blessing, and it's as if God said, "Okay. But here's what it looks like outside of my design."

To better understand the devastation of life outside of God's design, look at the summary statements of humanity's consequences. Next to each statement, record a "memory" or two from Genesis 1–2 that demonstrates how God's design has now been tainted. I did the first one for you as an example.

SUMMARY STATEMENT	MEMORY FROM GENESIS 1-2
Pain while bringing forth (and bringing up) children	Growing a family was framed up with only blessing in Genesis 1:28: "God blessed them, and God said to them, "Be fruitful, multiply, fill the earth . . ."
Division and oppression in relationships	(Gen. 2:22-25)
Land that fights against human efforts	(Gen. 1:11-12)
Work that is frustrating, burdensome, and unfulfilling	(Gen. 2:15)

How do you relate to these aspects of the curse?

LET'S LOOK AT GENESIS 3:20-24.

As Genesis 3 comes to a close with such deadly consequence, God gives Adam and Eve three blessings to prepare them for living in a sin-laden world: a hope for life, a covering for life, and a life-giving boundary.

1. A hope for life – Genesis 3:20

We've been calling Eve "Eve" this whole time, but up until this point, Scripture has just called her "woman" or "wife." Also, we've been calling Adam "Adam," but Scripture has been saying "man." The Hebrew word for *man* is "adam," and that's why we (and Bible translators) call the man "Adam."[3] (I mean, who knows. Maybe he preferred going by the name Cornelius.) But a beautiful thing happens at this point in the narrative. Adam, who has been entrusted with naming all the animals (see 2:20), names his wife.

Why does Adam name her "Eve"?

How was this probably an honoring experience for Eve?

In their most recent interaction, Adam spoke about Eve with blame. But Eve's name reminds us a bit of their pre-sin interaction when Adam spoke about her using poetry.

Why could we say this was an act of faith in God's promise in Genesis 3:15?

Adam and Eve were in this situation because they doubted God's word. But here, Adam seems to intentionally associate Eve with God's promise to send a snake-crushing son through woman.

2. A covering for life – Genesis 3:21

Consider for a moment the difference between Adam and Eve and God. God created the world with just His word, while Adam and Eve can barely make clothes for themselves, even when they borrow leaves God made. They are in need of a covering, and they can't make it themselves.

> **How is God's covering for Adam and Eve better than the coverings they made for themselves in verse 7?**

> **How would God have provided these coverings? (Hint: Look back at Gen. 2:19-20.) How do you imagine this experience impacted Adam and Eve?**

> **What do God's actions say about the seriousness of sin and what it truly takes to cover shame? What event is foreshadowed by this action?**

> **What does it say about God that He clothed them rather than sending them away in shame?**

Leaves are terrible clothes. (If you don't believe me, go try to make a dress using the foliage of your nearest tree.) They will turn brown, break down, and Adam and Eve would be back to naked pretty quickly. But how were they supposed to know that? They'd never needed clothes before. God, who had always provided for them, provided yet again, using something more substantial: the skins of animals. If you remember, Adam named all the animals! He was familiar with each and every one. But there was only one way for Adam and Eve to get clothing that would last and truly cover them. Before this moment, nothing had ever died. God was laying the groundwork for them to associate sin with death. Perhaps every time Adam and Eve got dressed, they pondered this. God's story teaches us that for sinners to be truly covered, death must occur.

3. A life-giving boundary – Genesis 3:22-24

In rejecting the design for this first home (and thus the Designer), Adam and Eve would now have what they thought they wanted: an opportunity to "be like God." They must make their own home.

Adam and Eve's forced exit from Eden can feel cruel, but whenever we are confused by God's Word or our circumstances, we must remember God's character.

What do you know to be true about Him from our study so far?

According to verse 22, why was their leaving an act of protection?

This first family stepped into a world tainted by sin, and our families endure this, too. If Adam and Eve looked back at the garden on their way out, it was clear that the way to the tree of life and to home with God would require someone coming under a sword. Who could do this?

Take heart, dear sister. God will keep His promise. The Eden promise is *the enemy of home will be destroyed*. God will make the way home, and He will conquer this evil serpent and the enemy of sin.

LOOK UP THE FOLLOWING VERSES TO SEE WHAT IS AHEAD.

Isaiah 25:6-8

Revelation 12:9

DAY FIVE
Where Are You?

After Adam and Eve sinned and hid, God asked them, "Where are you?" (Gen. 3:9) Counselor and writer K. J. Ramsey suggests in her book *This Too Shall Last* that this is perhaps an ongoing question He asks.[4] It's not that God didn't know where Adam and Eve were—or where we are—but the question is an invitation for us to notice where we are.

Have we gone into hiding over the shame of our sin? Our shame testifies: *I am not where I ought to be*. We feel naked and disgraced, unable to cover ourselves adequately. Maybe we reach for good deeds, perfectionism, distraction, or denial, but at the end of the day, it's all fig leaves. Such things cannot truly cover us. But God's invitation to us is "Come home." He alone can cover us because He alone has truly conquered the shame of sin through Jesus!

Are we longing for what only God can offer? The pangs of spiritual homesickness are like alerts from our soul's GPS: *I am not where I long to be*. That's why God's invitation is such a welcoming one: "Come home." He alone can bring us home.

On the final study day of each week, I'll share with you a letter from a fellow sister in Christ. As she shares her story of home, I hope it will help you better understand God's story of home, help reveal where you are, and assist you in finding your way home to Him.

Dear Sister,

Home and the feeling of homesickness has always been kind of a theme in my life, and the feeling of not really belonging anywhere. I'm adopted from China, so that's probably where part of it comes from. I don't know for what reasons my biological parents gave me away, and why I ended up in the orphanage. I don't feel Chinese since I'm raised with Western values. But I also don't feel Dutch since I don't look the same as my Dutch family.

God blessed me by giving me the two loveliest parents. They raised me with their whole hearts and all the love they have. They also raised me in faith, letting me know that I have a heavenly Father who watches over me and holds me in His hand and that I belong in His kingdom, as His daughter. He knows where I come from and for what reasons my life came to be, and He has been there with me all the time. I belong with Him as His daughter! :)

Like Psalm 139:13-14 (KJV) beautifully says: "For Thou hast possessed my reins: thou hast covered me in my mother's womb. I will praise thee; for I am fearfully and wonderfully made: Marvellous are Thy works; And that my soul knoweth right well."

Even though (if all is well) there are many things and people to love on earth, it's nothing close to how much God loves us and wants us with Him! That thought gives me so much strength and peace! We are wandering the earth but our home—our true home where we belong—is with Him.

God is great!

— **JADE VAN DER ZALM**, *illustrator, the Netherlands* —

Jade illustrated my children's book, The Story of Home!

Use the space below (or your own journal) to respond to this letter. You may want to use the following questions to guide your response.

What thoughts and feelings are you experiencing as you consider this sister's story?

What from her letter most resonates with you and why?

How does her story help you understand God's story of home, reveal where you are, or help you find your way home to Him?

The First Home

In the beginning,
God used His word
To turn a bunch of nothing
Into land, sea, beasts, birds

Man was created by God
And was created for home
Look how God provided
Look how man was known

He made us to bear His image
To point the world to Him
At first this purpose seemed plenty
Until the deceiver stepped in

"Did God really say?"
The serpent questioned the Word
It made us start to wonder
Did we really hear what we heard?

Sin promised to give
But really it was a crook
It intruded our home
And took, and took, and took

God punished but promised
A Seed would be sown
To provide our salvation
To make our way home

Seeking a homeland

session two

By faith Abraham . . . went out,
even though he did not know where he was going.

HEBREWS 11:8

Sin made its home in every human heart—the horrific inheritance
from our "first parents," Adam and Eve. And yet, God still desired
to be with people. He set His favor on one particular man—a guy
named Abram (later Abraham). Abraham was an old guy with
no kids, but God offered Abraham a promise of home, and this
big promise was made up of a few promises. He promised to give
Abraham a place and to make him a people who would enjoy God's
blessing and pass God's blessing along to the world. Abraham
believed God—even to the point of being willing to pick up and
leave everything familiar. These kinds of actions cause us to look to
these Bible guys as big pillars of faith, but we need to keep in mind
they were human, just like us.

Abraham didn't know where he was going, and he didn't know
what God was doing. Rather than settle for a worldly experience of
home, Abraham looked ahead to the home God promised. Except
of course when Abraham didn't trust God at all and took matters
into his own hands. (See? Very human.) But despite all his failings,
God kept His promise to Abraham and passed it down to his son,
and his grandson, and his great grandsons, ensuring them that He
would be with them wherever they were. God's promise was not
just to bring them home; His promise was to *be* their home.

VIEWER GUIDE

session two

Watch the Session Two video. Use this page to take notes, capture quotes, or doodle some thoughts from the video teaching session.

Cain - first murder

Noah - Genesis 9 - grandson of Adam

Genesis 9-12 - Abram + family - land - nation - blessing

Jacob married Israel

Genesis 28 10-19 Bethel House of God

To access the video teaching sessions, use the instructions in the back of your Bible study book.

DISCUSSION/REFLECTION QUESTIONS

If you're doing this study with a group, be ready to discuss these questions during your time together. (If you're leading a group, check out the leader guide at lifeway.com/comehome to help you prepare.) If you're doing this study solo, use the following questions to reflect on what you've heard in the video teaching.

1 What is one thing in the video teaching that stood out to you? Why?

2 What does it mean to walk by faith? How did Abraham display it?

3 Would you say you are currently walking by faith? If not, why not? If so, what is the evidence?

4 Jacob had a life-changing encounter with God at Bethel. What is one "Bethel" moment you've had in your relationship with God? How did it impact you?

5 What does it mean that God was not just bringing Israel home but was *being* Israel's home? How is He doing the same for you?

6 Why is the journey home an important part of going home? What's your favorite part of the journey?

7 Like Jacob, do you ever find yourself fighting to secure your own blessings rather than trusting God to keep His promises? Explain.

8 If someone asked you what you learned in our time together today, what would you say?

DAY ONE
Trace the Promises

READ GENESIS 12:1-3. **God offered Abraham a promise of home, and this big promise was made up of a few promises. Look for the following three promises, and check the box when you find each one.**

☑ **Land**

☑ **Nation**

☐ **Two-way blessing (Abram's family will be blessed; Abram's family will be a blessing)**

Which aspect of God's promise of home to Abraham appeals to you the most? Why?

Land
Blessing

Interestingly, God repeated these promises to Abraham several times. (Since God later changed Abram's name to Abraham, we'll use that name throughout the lesson.) God also repeated them to Abraham's son Isaac, and Isaac's son Jacob (later Israel). Let's examine the repetitions and see what we can learn.

If you feel a nudge to take one of these options but find your inner perfectionist bullying you, here's a reminder: God has shaped your seasons and your days. It is wise to honor the limitations of your season. The options will help you do that and allow you to still meaningfully interact with His Word.

Psst. If this starts to feel like too much (and it may, if you are unfamiliar with this part of Genesis, find it overwhelming to skim or flip several pages, or are in a season of intense caregiving and thus lots of interruptions), here are two options to protect you from being overwhelmed:

1. Only complete the starred (★) options. This will give you a solid overview of God's repeated promise to this family.

2. Spread this content out over a day or two. After all, this study contains five study days after each teaching session, so there's a bit of flex time within your week. Take it if you need it.

ABRAHAM

READ GENESIS 12:6-9.

Context: By faith in God to keep His promise, Abram did what God asked, and he left his homeland at seventy-five years old. Abram arrived in the land of Canaan when God appeared to him yet again.

Why do you think God repeated His promise at this point?

To remind Abram of what he promised

What aspects of the promise (land, nation, two-way blessing) were repeated or emphasized?

The land

What do you notice that's new or significant?

Building the altar

READ GENESIS 13:14-17.

Context: Abram brought his nephew Lot with him to the land of promise. Because both men had lots of livestock and herdsmen, they needed to separate. Abram graciously allowed Lot to choose which portion of the land he wanted. Lot chose the land near Sodom. It looked as lush as the garden in Eden, but it was next to a city that had become known for sin. After Lot and Abram went their separate ways, God spoke to Abram.

Why do you think God repeated His promise at this point?

What aspects of the promise were repeated or emphasized?

The land to his offspring

What do you notice that's new or significant?

★READ GENESIS 15:1-7,18.

Context: After Abram rescued Lot from nearby kings and received a blessing from a mysterious priest-king named Melchizedek, God appeared to him in a vision. Abram was still childless, and he wasn't sure how God was going to fulfill His promises.

Why do you think God repeated His promise at this point?

What aspects of the promise were repeated or emphasized?

What do you notice that's new or significant?

★READ GENESIS 17:1-8,15-21.

Context: At ninety-nine years old, Abram had one son, Ishmael, but this son was conceived outside of God's design. In an attempt to fulfill God's promise on their own, Abram's wife Sarai told Abram to have a child with her servant Hagar. Hagar, who had no power over this couple, looked at Sarai with contempt, and Sarai's resulting mistreatment caused Hagar to flee. God met Hagar in the desert and promised Hagar that He would make a great nation from her child. God saw her, and He cared for her and her child. Even still, this child was not the way God would fulfill His promise to Abram. Sarai, already ninety years old, would have a child.

Why do you think God repeated His promise at this point?

What aspects of the promise were repeated or emphasized?

What do you notice that's new or significant?

ISAAC

★ *READ GENESIS 26:2-6.*

Context: Isaac and his wife Rebekah had twins, Esau and Jacob. Their family dynamic was difficult because of favoritism on the parents' part, trickery on Jacob's part, and godlessness on Esau's part. (See Heb. 12:16.) There was a famine in the land of promise (Canaan), so Isaac went to Gerar, which was located in the land of the Philistines. (The most famous Philistine you've probably heard of is Goliath!) God appeared to Isaac in a dream, repeating the promise He made to Abraham and telling Isaac not to go to Egypt. He should "sojourn" (ESV) or stay "as an alien" (CSB) in Gerar.

Why do you think God repeated His promise at this point?

What aspects of the promise were repeated or emphasized?

What do you notice that's new or significant?

★ *READ GENESIS 26:24.*

Context: In Gerar, Isaac repeated his father's history but in a bad way. Rather than trust God to protect him in enemy territory, Isaac asked his wife Rebekah to lie to the ruler of the Philistines, Abimelech (which is a title, not a name[1]), and say she was his sister. Apparently, in this culture, men might so desire a beautiful woman that they would kill her husband in order to have her. In the past, Abraham asked Sarah to pretend to be his sister in order to protect his life (Gen. 12:10-20; 20:1-18), and Isaac asked the same thing of Rebekah. Interestingly, Abimelech displayed more character than Isaac (perhaps this was the same Abimelech as the one who interacted with Abraham in Genesis 20!), and Rebekah was spared from the local men. Interestingly, God continued to bless Isaac despite his distrust.

Why do you think God repeated His promise at this point?

What aspects of the promise were repeated or emphasized?

What do you notice that's new or significant?

READ GENESIS 28:3-6. *(Note: In all of today's examples except this one, God repeated His promises. But here, Isaac repeated God's promise to his son, Jacob.)*

Context: After tricking Esau and Isaac and thus stealing Esau's blessing, Jacob needed to flee from his brother, Esau, who was angry enough to plot Jacob's murder. Cunningly, Rebekah encouraged Isaac to send Jacob away so he could find a wife among Isaac's relatives. Before Jacob left, Isaac spoke God's promise over him.

Why do you think Isaac repeated God's promise at this point?

What aspects of the promise were repeated or emphasized?

What do you notice that's new or significant?

JACOB

READ GENESIS 28:13-15.

Context: This is the text we studied in our video teaching time. Jacob left his homeland with the stated purpose to find a wife among his father's relatives, but that was probably secondary to getting away from Esau. On the way, Jacob spent the night in a place he later named Bethel ("house of God"), and God spoke to him in a dream.

Why do you think God repeated His promise at this point?

What aspects of the promise were repeated or emphasized?

What do you notice that's new or significant?

★READ GENESIS 35:9-12

Context: In an event that mirrors Jacob's experience with God decades before at Bethel, God called Jacob to go to Bethel and live there with his growing family. When Jacob arrived, God repeated His promise, including the name change to Israel (Gen. 32:24-28), which would come to define the twelve tribes that came from Jacob's sons. After they left Bethel, his beloved wife Rachel, who'd already given Jacob his favorite son, Joseph, died giving birth to his youngest son, Benjamin.

Why do you think God repeated His promise at this point?

What aspects of the promise were repeated or emphasized?

What do you notice that's new or significant?

Why do you think God repeated His promise so often?

My husband always laughs at me because I say, "Life is long." Of course, life is short, but I bet you also understand the feeling that life is long! I think this is a big reason why God was so faithful to repeat His promises to Abraham, Isaac, and Jacob. These men lived a lot of life, and there had to be moments when it felt as if God was dragging His feet. But God's plans always unfold right on time, and they always unfold perfectly according to His promises.

Do you ever need to hear God's promises repeated?

DAY TWO

Our Keeper and The Promise Keeper

In Genesis 28, God repeated His promise of home to Jacob/Israel. It amazed Jacob, compelling him to exclaim, "Surely the LORD is in this place, and I did not know it!" He named the place "Bethel," or the "house of God." Jacob didn't just *hear* about the promise of home that night; he *experienced* a piece of it.

> LOOK UP GENESIS 28:15. **If you're comfortable writing in your Bible, underline or highlight the verse. What part of it stands out to you the most? Why?**

The verse offers an enhancement to the original promise to Abraham. This family would have God's attentive presence. They were promised God's watchful gaze. God would be their Keeper, their Guardian.

Different translations provide different English words to communicate the Hebrew root *shamar*, which means "to keep, watch, preserve."[2] Consider the two translations below to get a sense of this special word:

- "Behold, I am with you and *will keep you* wherever you go . . . " (ESV)

- "Look, I am with you and *will watch over you* wherever you go . . . " (CSB)

The word makes me think of parenting young children at a pool or a crowded place like the zoo or a state fair. It speaks to vigilance, that "ready to act" posture, that alertness that can only be motivated by deep and unyielding love—the constant readiness that drains the life out of you and feels like total exhaustion when you finally get to fall into bed at the end of the day.

What personal experiences does this word call to mind?

Shamar is not a casual promise. *Shamar* pushes us humans to our limits. Of course, God has no limits.

Let's look at another interesting place this word shows up—back in Genesis 4, right after the first murder.

In Genesis 4:1-10, we have the story where Adam and Eve's son Cain killed his brother Abel. *READ GENESIS 4:9* **and write it below.** (Circle) **the word that you think is from the Hebrew root** *shamar.*

We hear the haunting echoes of Cain's word with every wound humanity commits against one another: *"Am I my brother's keeper?"* Am I supposed to *"shamar"* him?

Cain's question was rhetorical and perhaps even a snide reference to Abel's job as a keeper of sheep. Even still, how would you respond to his question, "Am I my brother's keeper?"

This is why God's promise is good news: What men and women and kids fail to do for one another, God does not fail to do.

- Abraham failed to watch over Sarah—but God kept watch (Gen. 12:10-20; 20:1-18).

- Sarah and Abraham failed to watch over Hagar—but God kept watch (Gen. 16).

- Isaac failed to watch over Rebekah—but God kept watch (Gen. 26:7-11).

- Jacob and Esau failed to watch over one another—but God kept watch (Gen. 25:29-34; 27).

- Joseph's brothers failed to watch over him—but God kept watch (Gen. 37).

Can you think of any other examples like this in Scripture?

All the while, God was their keeper.

God's people have been clinging to this promise for generations. In fact, Psalm 121, which says in verse 5a, "The LORD is your keeper" (ESV), was likely sung by travelers who looked to the distant hills of Jerusalem as they journeyed "home" to the city that held God's holy temple. (More on that soon!)

TAKE A MOMENT TO READ PSALM 121 **and answer the following questions.**

What evidence do you see in Psalm 121 of God's limitlessness?

Verse 7 says that God will keep us from all evil. Based on the examples we've studied this week (like Sarah, Hagar, Rebekah, and Joseph), why would it be foolish to think God has promised we'll experience perfect safety at every moment?

How do the Genesis narratives help you understand what it looks like for God to keep watch over His people?

God's promise to keep careful and loving watch over His children still belongs to God's people today. The promise doesn't mean He creates a magical force field around us that makes us immune to sin's power and devastation. We're not always protected from the trouble evil causes in our world. But we are protected from the eternal damnation evil brings. God will be with us all our days and will bring us home to Him. Think about the example of Joseph: God did not spare him from being sold by his brothers or from being falsely accused or from prison, but God was with him in the foreign land of Egypt. God placed His favor on Joseph again and again and used Joseph's position to rescue his family from starvation! Truly, the Lord was Joseph's keeper.

To close, let's look a little further into God's story of home. It's a bit of a spoiler, but you probably saw it coming: Through Jesus, God is forming a new family—a family that will learn to love as God loves. A family of keepers.

READ 1 JOHN 3:1,11-18 **and answer the following questions.**

How does John refer to members of this early church in verse 1?

What message had this church heard from the beginning (v. 11)?

How is that true love for one another described in verses 16-17?

Based on these verses in 1 John 3, do you think Christians (children of God) are called to be their brothers' and sisters' keepers? Explain.

God's children are not perfect "keepers." At least not yet. But our God is a perfect Keeper. He will keep growing us into His image, and He will keep us in His careful gaze until we are fully with Him forever.

DAY THREE

The Promised Home

Hebrews 11 is known as "The Faith Chapter." I will never not know this because when I was in my later elementary school years, I competed in Bible Drill, a Bible memory competition, and certain Bible facts are forever seared into my memory. When the caller shouted "Faith Chapter!" I would step across the line, knowing that if called upon, I'd need to give the correct answer: Hebrews 11. This question didn't stress me out too badly, but sometimes the caller would say things like, "Obadiah," and then I'd be scrambling to find the smallest and most obscure book ever. (Go try to find Obadiah right now, and you'll see what I mean. Also, pretend you are nine years old and YOU HAVE THIRTY SECONDS to locate it.)

For lots of kids, Bible Drill was a fun, exciting program, but my attentive parents soon discerned it was—how shall I say this—not for me. Competition is like a foreign substance in my body, and I am prone to allergic reactions. If you've ever seen a person wearing a shirt to a sporting event that says, "I just hope both teams have fun," you've seen my life verse. What I lack in competitive zeal I make up for in anxious energy. When asked to compete in any way, a little tornado swirls within me and threatens to come out. I suppose this explains the post-Bible Drill barfing.

Looking back, I know what caused the anxiety cyclones: I was worried I would fail. That I wouldn't measure up. The whole thing threatened my "good girl" persona. What if I fell on my face and everyone could see I wasn't as good as advertised? A program that was designed to train me to know God's Word went squirrely in my mind, and I internalized it as anti-gospel. I felt being good enough was on me. But the Bible teaches something like this: *God is good. You are not good, but you are loved by God, and you need Him. By faith, you can belong to God. Your value is found in Him, not in yourself. As you walk with Him in faith, He will shape you to look like Him—and that is good.*

Hebrews 11 is not merely a Bible Drill question. It is a chapter jam-packed with people who were *not good enough* but who believed God's promises and found that He was good enough. It begins with this definition of faith: "Now faith is the reality of what is hoped for, the proof of what is not seen."

> The CSB footnotes help us see that reality *can also be translated as* assurance, *and* proof *can also be translated as* conviction. *Sometimes synonyms help our brains chew on the meaning of a verse and understand it a bit better, so you may want to reread the verse with those two words instead.*[3]

The chapter continues with what some Bible teachers have cleverly called "The Hall of Faith." It lists men and women from the Old Testament who responded to the Lord in faith. They are a "great cloud of witnesses" who encourage us to run the race set before us, looking to Jesus, the founder and perfecter of our faith (Heb. 12:1-2). They testify to us that we can cling to God's promises right now.

With that in mind, let's look at what Hebrews 11 has to say about our guy Abraham and his wife, Sarah.

READ HEBREWS 11:8-12 and answer the following questions.

When God called Abraham to go to a new place, He did not specify the location. What do you imagine went through Abraham's heart and mind as he pondered this calling? (And by the way, does this humanize him for you? We easily forget to view Bible characters as human beings!)

What kind of dwelling did Abraham, Isaac, and Jacob live in and why?

Who created the home Abraham was looking ahead to, and how is that home described?

When Sarah looked at herself, she saw an old lady, making God's promise seem impossible. But when she looked to Him, what did she see?

Why do you think verse 12 describes Abraham "as good as dead"? How does this enhance your understanding of God's ability to keep His promises? How does this enhance your understanding of the power of God's blessing to produce life in and through those He blesses?

Living in tents? Waiting on a baby in the geriatric years? It's hard to see the logic in the way Abraham and Sarah's lives unfolded. When we look at our lives from a human perspective, sometimes God's promises make no sense. All we can see are the limits. But God Himself has no limits, and this is one of the reasons we can trust Him to fulfill His promises!

READ HEBREWS 11:13-16. **As you read, look up any words you'd like to better understand.**

God promised Abraham (1) land, (2) nation, and (2) blessing that goes both ways, but verse 13 reminds us that Abraham did not receive this in full while he was alive. Instead, he waved to God's promise from a distance and declared himself a foreigner on earth. Home was a guarantee—but not here, not yet. Rather than put all his hope in an immediate home, Abraham looked ahead to a better place.

TAKE A PEEK AT THE DEFINITION OF FAITH IN HEBREWS 11:1. **In your own words, describe how Abraham is an example of faith.**

Everyone who belongs to the Lord is "seeking a homeland," like Abraham. How do you sense this longing in your life?

Verse 13 talks about greeting the things God promised from a distance. What might it look like in your life to set aside worldly instincts and instead operate in view of the home God has promised? *(For example, when I choose to risk personal comfort in order to invest in my eternal home by telling others about Jesus, I am greeting the things God promised.)*

What has God prepared for us and how does this reward encourage us as "temporary residents on the earth"?

In the age of social media and Pinterest® and home makeover shows, it's easy to think of our homes with only the present in mind. Our homes can easily become spaces not rooted in faith—places where we perform, prove, and/or protect ourselves.

Let's apply a Hebrews 11 view of home to some modern-day home examples.

How should a *homemaker* who has faith in God's promise view home?

How should a *homeowner* who has faith in God's promise view home?

How should a *homebody* ("a person who likes spending time at home rather than going out with friends or traveling to different places"[4]) who has faith in God's promise view home?

When verse 16 says Abraham and others desired a "better" place, the word *better* means "of a more excellent or effective type or quality."[5] So, when by faith we long for something better for our homes, we are looking toward something better than a remodel, better than hosting friends, better than a rent check. We are longing for what God alone has promised to His children: a forever-beautiful home with our forever-loving Father alongside our forever-loved family.

If your home is full of pain right now, you can have faith that something better is ahead. Even if your home situation right now is wonderful, you can have faith something better is ahead. Here's the truth: both the bad and the good point to the promises ahead.

My daughter loves our home and often worries we'll move. Something in her knows that earthly homes do not offer the permanence we desire. But here's what I tell her, and I know that it's true: "Everything you love about our home is just a glimmer of the better home God is building."

Sister, whatever story of home surrounds you, wave to the promises ahead. Home is not here, not yet, but it is coming, and it's yours all the same.

DAY FOUR

The Promised Offering

It may surprise you that God's promises of home to Abraham, Isaac, and Jacob pop up a few times in the New Testament (Luke 19:9; Acts 7; Rom. 9–11; Heb. 11). (Lest we ever think the Old Testament is irrelevant to our lives, the New Testament writers bring it up over and over again!) God's promises to Abraham were significant before Jesus came to live a perfect life on earth, die a punishing death, and return to life—and they are even more significant after all that happened. God's promise of home to Abraham, Isaac, and Jacob is significant for Christians today—significant for you—because it all points to Jesus.

Let's consider what Paul wrote pretty firmly to the church of Galatia. They had forgotten the nature of the gospel—that God's rescue for sinners comes by faith, not by people doing stuff. Paul was like, "Um, absolutely not."

This was the situation: Christians from a Jewish background were trying to impose Jewish laws on non-Jewish Christians, and it was warping their understanding of the gospel. Even Peter, a leader in the church and one of Jesus's disciples who truly understood the gospel, got tangled up in this distortion. He acted as if people needed to do things to truly be Christians, rather than simply cling to what Christ has done.

It's actually pretty easy to slip into this kind of thinking. Modern-day examples might be believing people need to clean up their behavior before they can come to Christ, or believing folks must read their Bibles, pray every day, and be baptized in order to truly belong to the Lord.

Paul, a fierce defender of the gospel, spoke to these Jewish Christians in a way they could understand—by bringing up Abraham. For these people, connection to Abraham was everything! After all, he was the original receiver of the promise. The twelve tribes of Israel descended from him. All Jewish people sought to trace their lineage back to one of those tribes so they could be connected with him. This would make each of them truly a part of the family—a "son of Abraham."

But as they lost sight of the gospel, they misunderstood God's family, and they misunderstood God's promise. We are prone to do this, too.

READ GALATIANS 3:5-9.

What makes someone truly a "son of Abraham"?

What does this text teach you about the family of God?

Look over the repeated promises below. In each verse, (circle) the word *offspring*. (By the way, this word literally means "seed."[6])

- Genesis 12:7 – "The LORD appeared to Abram and said, 'To your offspring I will give this land.' So, he built an altar there to the LORD who had appeared to him."

- Genesis 13:15 – "for I will give you and your offspring forever all the land that you see."

- Genesis 17:8 – "And to you and your future offspring I will give the land where you are residing—all the land of Canaan—as a permanent possession, and I will be their God."

The Jewish Christians in Galatia believed they were Abraham's offspring because they were circumcised (as God commanded Abraham in Gen. 17) and therefore, the recipients of the promise. In their minds those who were not Abraham's offspring were not able to receive the promise. In other words, they believed God's promise of home belonged to those who made themselves Abraham's sons through following the law, rather than believing the gospel, which says we can only come to the Father through Jesus (John 14:6).

Paul was having none of this. His arguments in Galatians were designed to show those believers how God's promises to Abraham actually point to Jesus.

Here's what he said in Galatians 3:16:

> Now the promises were spoken to Abraham and to his seed. He does not say "and to seeds," as though referring to many, but referring to one, and to your seed, who is Christ.

Interestingly, Paul emphasized that the promises were given to a person, not a group—to a particular offspring, through whom all the promises would be fulfilled! Yes, God would give Abraham many, many offspring, but the promise would come through one offspring: Jesus.

Go back to the repeated promises on the previous page, and every time you see the words "your offspring" write "Jesus" above them.

LOOK UP MATTHEW 1:1-16. **What three names do you notice in verse 1?**

What name finishes the family line in verse 16?

How does the outcome of this lineage give evidence of Paul's claim in Galatians 3:16?

Abraham, Isaac, and Jacob didn't have access to this God-designed "blueprint." How does seeing this genealogy increase your faith to press into God's promises even when you aren't sure how He'll fulfill them?

Don't miss this: God's promises to Abraham, Isaac, and Jacob are fulfilled in Jesus; He is the way that these promises are fulfilled to all of God's children. Through Jesus, anyone who looks to Him in faith can become a child of God and receive all of God's promises of home.

LOOK UP 2 CORINTHIANS 1:20 **and write it below.**

When we come across any of God's promises in the Bible, we can immediately think about Jesus! Jesus will help us understand the true meaning of God's promises. When we don't view God's promises in light of Jesus, things can get tricky. In fact, when we misunderstand the gospel, we misunderstand God's family, and we are prone to harm God's family and muddle one another's understanding of Jesus being the only way home. For example, if we misunderstand that we come into God's family by faith in Jesus, we might think we belong to God because we behave a certain way—leading us to treat people with different behaviors as outsiders. We might mistreat these "outsiders" or mislead them into thinking that to be part of the family, they must act the way we want them to act.

> **Do you ever notice this kind of anti-gospel thinking within yourself, like Paul saw in the Galatians? Do you ever notice it within other Christians you know? Explain.**

When we cling to the truth of the gospel, it protects our temporary homes and invests in our eternal family. For example, when I know that my true home is in God alone and that He is forming my true family, I am free to pursue relationships with people whom others are tempted to judge or overlook. Because of the gospel, my social status is no longer the concern that it once was. Instead, I now concern myself with the true family I have in Christ and the beautiful invitation I get to extend to others: "Come home."

> **What are some other practical ways we can "cling to the true gospel" in our relationships?**

DAY FIVE

Where Are You?

A big theme in this part of God's story of home is fractured relationships. People refuse to be one another's "keeper." Parents have favorites. Siblings hate one another.

Home is never just a place; it's always people, too. And it's not just the people but the peace we deeply desire to have with these people. All the ways we lack place, people, and peace is evidence that we, like Abraham, Isaac, and Jacob, aren't home yet.

Hebrews 11:13 says that Abraham, Isaac, and Jacob "all died in faith, although they had not received the things that were promised. But they saw them from a distance, greeted them, and confessed that they were foreigners and temporary residents on the earth." In a way, this was their way of answering God's question that reverberated from Eden, "Where are you?"

They said in faith, "I am not home yet," and our own fractured relationships echo this. Often, paying attention to our soul's GPS invites us to cling more tightly to God's promises and walk in faith that He will answer them.

I want to share with you a letter from a fellow sister in Christ. As she shares her story of home, I hope it will point you to God's story of home and give you an opportunity to notice where you are—not home yet.

Dear Sister,

I stepped into my bedroom and clicked on the light. Everything was exactly as it had been that morning—books askew on my nightstand, the laundry basket full of unfolded clothes.

I breathed in the stillness and stared at my bed. It felt tainted now. Filthy. Dirty.

I knew I needed to sleep, and that wouldn't happen on the floor. So I pulled back my duvet and lay on the very edge of my bed. I didn't want to even touch my husband's side of the bed. The void was massive. He should have been there. But he wasn't.

He was with her.

And now everything was different.

Everything had changed.

After my husband's unfaithfulness was exposed, I lost everything. First came the shattering, as everything sordid came to light. And then?

Everything precious began to unravel.

My husband was a pastor, so with news of his affair came a letter of resignation to our church. As we were living overseas as missionary church planters, this led to canceled visas. Next, I watched as my dream home was boxed up; treasured items were sold or given away, suitcases were packed, and one-way tickets back to America were purchased.

I lost my home, my place of belonging, my church, my neighbors, my source of income, my place of ministry, my calling to the mission field . . . my dreams. We had arrived in Scotland four years earlier brimming with joy, dreams, and so much hope. We returned to America with shame, grief, and a broken family.

HOME is my favorite word, my favorite concept. I love the idea of belonging, of knowing and being known. Of safety, security, familiarity, and embrace. Home is unconditional love—even when at our worst, home continues to hope and hold firm.

In one fell swoop, I lost HOME. The rug was pulled from under my feet, and I felt like a wanderer in the world. My marriage and my family never recovered from this shattering. My story doesn't tie up with a pretty bow. Instead, I faced the ultimate rejection as my husband—who had become my home in so many ways—decided to leave our family forever.

But here's what I've found to be true: in the world, I was HOME-LESS, but in God, I found my ultimate HOME. He is the Refuge I turned to. He tucked me in close, under the shadow of His wings (Ps. 91). He knows me, fully and completely (Ps. 139).

continued

He loves me, no matter what (Rom. 8). He is my Safe Place (Prov. 18:10), my Provider (Matt. 6), my Friend (John 15), and a perfect Father to my children (Ps. 68:5). He brought me in from the cold and embraced me when my home lay shattered.

Dear sister, God is our perfect HOME. We can rest, fully known, fully loved, and welcomed in. So open the door, click on the light, and enjoy the comforts of home. He is our eternal Dwelling Place, and underneath are His everlasting arms (Deut. 33:27).

— RACHEL SETLIFFE, *Founder and Director of Restored Home, Scotland*

Use the space below (or your own journal) to respond to this letter. You may want to use the following questions to guide your response.

What thoughts and feelings are you experiencing as you consider this sister's story?

What from her letter most resonates with you and why?

How does her story help you understand God's story of home, reveal where you are, or help you find your way home to Him?

Seeking a Homeland

Outside of Eden
Sin grew
It changed what we did,
Corrupted what we knew

We invited the enemy
We entertained our foe
Until what God said was good
Didn't really seem so

We longed for home
Deep in our hearts,
But sin muddled the way
Infiltrating every part

God kept the course
While we waffled and waned
So prone to wander
Yet God stayed the same

He set His favor on Abram
Isaac and Jacob too
Their course filled with blessings
That affect me and you

It points to the Redeemer
The One God said He'd send
It points to our true home
Which we barely comprehend

Their days were a journey
And so, of course, are ours
We too live lives unsettled
Fighting against sin's power

But here's a big point
A promise to which we cling
God is with us always
It is a guaranteed thing

God does what He says
He always keeps His word
No matter how sin hisses
His promises are confirmed

It was true for them,
It's true for you;
God promised to bring us home,
That's exactly what He'll do

going

home

session three

Lord, through all generations, you have been our home!

PSALM 90:1, NLT

Eventually Abraham's great-grandsons all wound up in Egypt. It's a long and dramatic story, but this is the detail you need for the story of home: Their family grew into a giant nation of people, and seeing them as a threat, Pharaoh enslaved them and sought to kill their sons. They were trapped in an unsafe home, but God was keeping watch. He offered miraculous protection to one of those baby boys, who grew to become the deliverer Pharaoh feared. His name was Moses. If there's anyone acquainted with the longing for home, it's him. Moses never really had a place to call home. Even when God's people were almost home to the promised land, Moses wasn't allowed to enter. But still, he penned these words in Psalm 90 (NLT): "Lord, through all the generations you have been our home!" One of the ways Moses experienced "home" was by meeting with God in the tabernacle, an Eden-reminiscent tent designed by God and built by men for the purpose of togetherness. Eventually, this tent became the temple, a permanent structure where God's presence would dwell in the promised land. This would be the closest to true home God's people had experienced since Eden.

Christine McCaul
Luke in the land

VIEWER GUIDE

session three

Watch the Session Three video. Use this page to take notes, capture quotes, or doodle some thoughts from the video teaching session.

Home is where I AM is !

Lord, Yahew

To access the video teaching sessions, use the instructions in the back of your Bible study book.

DISCUSSION/REFLECTION QUESTIONS

If you're doing this study with a group, be ready to discuss these questions during your time together. (If you're leading a group, check out the leader guide at **lifeway.com/comehome** to help you prepare.) If you're doing this study solo, use the following questions to reflect on what you've heard in the video teaching.

1   What is one thing in the video teaching that stood out to you? Why?

2   How was Moses's relationship with home complicated? Would you say you've had a complicated relationship with home? Explain.

3   God told Moses His name is "I AM WHO I AM." How would you explain what that means and how that name shapes how you see God?

I am who I am
yahew

4   How have you experienced God's compassion and faithful love in recent days?

5   What are some things that keep us from trusting God when He's calling us to move forward in life, home, ministry? Are you currently struggling with any of these? Explain.

6   Is it hard for you to accept that God did not permit Moses to enter the promised land? Explain.

7   Even though Moses did not enter the promised land, he lacked nothing when it came to receiving God's promise of home. How is this truth helpful for you when you do not receive what you desire?

8   If someone asked you what you learned in our time together today, what would you say?

DAY ONE

Togetherness With God, Part 1

Exodus 32 through 34 describes events that must've been very formative in Moses's life and gave him (and will give us) a much bigger understanding of God's promises of home. We'll look into these chapters the next couple of days.

Here's the setting: God's people, somewhat recently delivered from slavery in Egypt (like, under two years), were camped at Mount Sinai. Moses had gone up on Mount Sinai to receive the stone tablets upon which God had written "the law and commandments" for the people (Ex. 24:12). These instructions were an integral installment of God's promise because it offered a countercultural and God-honoring foundation for how the *nation* should live in the *land* they would possess. It would *bless* them and allow them to be a blessing.

But, receiving those instructions took a while. The people saw that Moses "delayed" (Ex. 32:1) coming down from the mountain, and they became what I call "spiritually itchy." They didn't understand what God was doing or what their human leader was doing. They became antsy and afraid. Who would lead them to their new home? Though their deliverance from Egypt had proved God's promises ("I will be with you; I will lead you home"), and Moses's leadership proved another ("Home is where I AM is"), they rebelled.

Rather than cling to what they knew about God, they created, in their own sinfulness, something that made sense to them. Of course, since it was created out of sinfulness, it was created with a distorted vision. You can't get home with distorted vision.

They said to Aaron (Moses's brother and coleader), "Come, make gods for us who will go before us because this Moses, the man who brought us up from the land of Egypt—we don't know what has happened to him (Ex. 32:1)."

The result: a golden calf, made from their own jewelry. Then they got busy worshiping it, probably mimicking the worship of the Egyptians, who they'd witnessed for hundreds of years.

Culturally, this makes no sense to us, but spiritually, it absolutely does. They were uncomfortable with trusting God to make the way, so they made their own way.

How is this situation like what Sarah and Abraham did when they tried to grow their family through Hagar (Gen. 16)?

How have you experienced this in your own life?

While Moses was with God on the mountain, God told him what the people were doing.

These events unfolded in a way that mirrors the Numbers 14 passage we talked about in the video teaching time. If you remember, God's people were afraid to enter the promised land and accused God of evil. In response to their rebellion, God told Moses He would pour out His wrath on the people, destroying them for their sin. Then, God would create a greater and mightier nation through Moses, and thus fulfill His promises through him. Of course, God could have done that and been just in doing so. But God's judgment moved Moses to intercede for the people, and God relented. Sinful people always need an intercessor. How else will they get home? Moses was modeling something bigger. He was foreshadowing the work of Jesus, who would intercede for sinners to make the way for them to be with God, to be home.

> *That event happened after this golden calf thing! Will God's people never learn?*

A similar thing happened in the golden calf situation.

> READ EXODUS 32:9-14. **What do you notice about how Moses interceded for the people?**

Moses interceded by appealing to God's character, reputation, and promises. God relented from the disaster, but the people's horrific idolatry was not without consequence. People died; God sent a plague. But there was something else that got everyone upset. What could be worse than death and sickness?

READ EXODUS 33:1-4. **What does this passage reveal about God's promises and how they would be fulfilled?**

What was the devastating news God gave Moses, and how was it described (vv. 3-4)? (You may want to look it up in a few translations.)

How did the people react to the news?

If you think about it, this is a natural consequence. God's people wanted to be led by a god of their own making, so in a sense, God was saying, "Okay. Go with your made-up gods." But once they remembered the true God, I AM, the people realized they had made a grievous error. They didn't want God's promises without God Himself! The information was disastrous and distressing.

Do you ever want God's promises without God's presence? If so, why?

In your own words, explain why the news about the absence of God's presence was so terrible.

But once again, Moses interceded.

LOOK UP EXODUS 33:15 **and write it below.**

Imagine how formative this was for Moses. He realized that God's presence is a greater treasure than a homeland, than a nation, than a blessing that goes both ways. For a man who'd never had a home and likely longed for it deeply and for many years, this is a significant lesson about home. Without God's presence, the stuff God promises loses its sweetness. It's just stuff. Home is where I AM is!

How does this challenge your view of home?

In your life, what does it look like to value God's presence above all else?

How did God respond to Moses's request in Exodus 33:17?

LOOK UP PSALM 139:23-24. **Use these verses and the space below to write a prayer to God. Ask God to use today's passages like an investigative tool to search you and to know your heart. Is there anything in you that grieves Him? Anything in you that is "spiritually itchy," something that's desperately trying to create a way that makes sense to you rather than clinging to God and what you know about Him? Notice that the end of verse 24 says, "lead me in the everlasting way." This feels like "true home" phrasing to me. Ask God to help you fight the enemy of sin here and now and to continue to lead you home.**

DAY TWO
Togetherness With God, Part 2

With is a powerful word, isn't it? Last session, we talked about how God promised Jacob that He would be with him. We also saw the impact of God's "withness" on Joseph as he endured many trials in Egypt. Interestingly, when God first commissioned Moses (the burning bush moment in Ex. 3), He said, "I will certainly be with you" (Ex. 3:12). Throughout Exodus, God's presence continued to be an important theme—and something Moses deeply desired as he did the work God set out for him.

Let's pick up where we left off yesterday in Exodus 33, right after God promised to go with them into the promised land (v. 17). At that point, Moses made a special request of God.

READ EXODUS 33:18-23.

What did Moses ask for and what was God's response?

What was the "but" of God's agreement?

What "covering" would God provide Moses to keep him safe?

The word *glory* is hard to define, but the Hebrew root implies a heaviness.[1] Think of a towel you've dropped in a pool. When you lift it up, it's heavy, dripping, and saturated with water. Similarly, God is dripping and saturated with wonderfulness. Moses asked to see God's glory, and Moses barely understood what he was asking for! It was more substantial, dripping, and saturated than he could grasp.

It was so "heavy" in fact, that Moses himself, the mediator, needed a mediator. He would need to be protected by a rock, covered by God's hand.

Lest you think this is weird and random, look up Matthew 21:42 and 1 Peter 2:4-7.

How is Jesus described in these passages?

How might these passages help us understand the scene in Exodus 33?

The rock reminds us of Christ the rock.[2] As John Piper said, God "is too great, too bright, too glorious, and we could not live if we saw him with unmediated directness. We must always have Christ our Mediator as a go-between."[3]

As God passed by, He caused all this goodness to pass before Moses, and He declared His glorious name ("I AM"!) alongside a list of character traits. If you ever forget what God is like, this is a text to remember.

LOOK UP EXODUS 34:6b-7 **and highlight it or bookmark it. Then, read the text below and take special note of the numbered characteristics:**

The LORD—the LORD is a [1] compassionate and [2] gracious God, [3] slow to anger and [4] abounding in faithful love and truth, [5] maintaining faithful love to a thousand generations, [6] forgiving iniquity, rebellion, and sin. [7] But he will not leave the guilty unpunished, bringing the consequences of the fathers' iniquity on the children and grandchildren to the third and fourth generation.

EXODUS 34:6b-7 (bracketed numbers added)

We probably feel fairly comfy with all of these traits—except #7. That sentence keeps us from framing this particular text and hanging it above the couch. What are we supposed to do with this part of God's character? How are we supposed to process #7 in light of #6? Just as Jesus expands our understanding of the rock part of the passage, He also expands our understanding of this part of the passage. Because Jesus is "the image of the invisible God" (Col. 1:15), looking at Jesus allows us to "see" God as He actually is—Someone who is able to both punish and forgive sin. How is this possible? Through the cross!

How was Jesus's death on the cross the way for God to both forgive and punish sin? Write down any thoughts you have.

We'll talk more about that later, but for now, let's get back to Moses. Despite this "covering with the rock" business, Moses experienced a relationship with God that was a glimmer of Eden's intimacy. Exodus 33:11 says that God "would speak with Moses face to face, just as a man speaks with his friend." From what will take place in the following verses, we understand the "face to face" phrase is not literal but a way to describe the closeness of their relationship.[4] These conversations took place in what Moses called the "tent of meeting," which was a precursor to the tabernacle.

> *READ EXODUS 25:8-9.* **What was God's purpose for the tabernacle He designed?**

This sacred space was like a movable worship spot, a way God could commune with His people no matter where He led them. For the first time since Eden, God's people could "walk" with Him in a tangible way.

> *READ EXODUS 31:1-11.* **How was God "with" His people during the building of the tabernacle?**

The tabernacle was carefully designed by God and built by God's people through God's inspiration. This group project had a clear purpose: *witness*. God commissioned them— like He commissioned Adam and Noah—to work on His behalf. God filled the tabernacle builders with His Spirit and gave them special skills so they could accomplish His work in His way.

Think of a time in which you experienced a heightened level of awareness that God was with you. How did that impact the way you lived in that season?

Are you currently living with an assured understanding of God's presence with you? If not, why not? If so, how is it affecting your life?

We could spend hours studying the tabernacle's design. (There are fifty chapters in the Bible dedicated to the tabernacle!)[5] God was incredibly specific, offering lots of glimmers of Eden, like imagery of cherubim, branches, and blossoms. It also included what Carl Laferton in his book, *The Garden, the Curtain, and the Cross*, memorably calls "a big KEEP OUT sign"—a veil—similar to the armed angels set up outside the garden of Eden after Adam and Eve's sin.[6] All the details taught God's people about God, and the end result of the tabernacle allowed God's people to meet with God through their mediators, Moses and the priests.

Here's why I'm telling you all this: the tabernacle looks back to Eden, but it also looks ahead to Jesus in at least three meaningful ways.

1. The tabernacle was the place where God would dwell. *LOOK UP JOHN 1:14.* (Note: The word *dwelt* literally means *tabernacled*.) How is Jesus the true tabernacle?

2. The tabernacle's veil points to Jesus. When the tabernacle tent was replaced with a more permanent structure, the temple, this veil remained. Only the high priest could go past this veil into the most holy place (or holy of holies) once a year (Lev. 16), functioning as a mediator between God and His people—that is, until Jesus. When Jesus died on the cross, this veil was ripped from top to bottom. (A heavenly tearing!) *LOOK UP 1 TIMOTHY 2:5–6.* How is Jesus the way to God?

3. As stated earlier, the tabernacle's "precursor," the tent of meeting, was a place where Moses would "see" God in a sense, talking with Him closely the way a man speaks with his friend (Ex. 33:11). Then, the tabernacle and later the temple were God-designed places for God's people to "see" Him as He actually is. *LOOK UP JOHN 14:8-9.* How is Jesus the way we "see" God?

The Moses passages we've looked at over the past couple of days teach us that God is with us, but Jesus takes all of these teachings and cranks up the volume! Truly, Jesus helps us "see" God the Father as He actually is, "for God was pleased to have all his fullness dwell in him" (Col. 1:19). Jesus is God, Jesus is God with us, Jesus is the Rock, Jesus is the true tabernacle/temple, Jesus is the Way to the Father, and Jesus is the Way home.

DAY THREE

Carried by God

Naming my children was a big deal to me. It's such pressure to, you know, DECIDE WHAT EVERYONE WILL CALL THESE HUMAN BEINGS FOR THEIR ENTIRE LIVES! I took it quite seriously.

(Meanwhile, we named our dog Ebenezer. I thought it sounded like a funny old guy name. We did not consider how this moniker would effectively compromise the beautiful line "here I raise my Ebenezer" from the hymn *Come Thou Fount* for all of our friends and family for all of time. Now when they hear this song, they visualize us holding up the dog Ebenezer like Simba in *The Lion King*. It's really not what the hymn writer had in mind. For this, we are sorry.)

My husband and I gave one of our sons a name with this rich meaning: carried by God. This son joined our family through adoption, and we are so, so, so glad to be his. We are also so, so, so aware that adoption means a child has lost a family. (Sometimes we Christians forget this part and only think about the family gained. For any sisters reading this who are adoptees, I know you have much to teach us. I know your story of home is complicated. God's promises are for you.)

We gave our son his name to help him view his story in light of God's story. Atop every school paper and every form in his life, he will scribble an important truth. To everyone who asks his name, he testifies, "I'm [carried by God]." Of course, we do not always understand the way God carries us; and in the midst of being carried, it's okay to question, to grieve, to receive His comfort. But it steadies us to know we can grapple with our pain and confusion from the safe position of being held in the arms of God.

Interestingly, Moses used this tender metaphor to describe the way God led His people. He said, "the LORD your God carried you as a man carries his son all along the way you traveled until you reached this place" (Deut. 1:31).

In your own words, describe what it is like to be carried.

Moses's words are an excerpt from a speech he gave to the new generation of Israelites as they prepared to say goodbye to Moses and enter the promised land under the leadership of Joshua.

By the way, the first five books of the Bible are called the Pentateuch and are commonly grouped together. They are considered to have been written almost exclusively by Moses under the inspiration of the Holy Spirit. The books contain more than narrative, but the included narratives take us from creation to the flood to the patriarchs—Abraham, Isaac, and Jacob/Israel—to Moses, the exodus, and the wilderness wanderings. By the time we get to the end of Deuteronomy, we find Moses instructing the new generation—the one given the promise when their parents before them doubted God (Num. 14:19-35)—so they can enter their new home knowing God, following God, loving God.

One of the things Moses did for this new generation is orient them in their history. As mentioned, they were the descendants of Israelites who, when God first brought them to the outskirts of the promised land, doubted God's power and goodness. And really, it went further than doubt. They almost considered Him an enemy!

READ THE FOLLOWING EXCERPT FROM DEUTERONOMY 1.

As you read:
- **Underline anything that reveals the character or response of the Israelites to God.**
- **Circle anything that reveals God's character or response to the Israelites.**

Don't forget: Moses is talking here!

²⁵ They took some of the fruit from the land in their hands, carried it down to us, and brought us back a report: 'The land the LORD our God is giving us is good.' ²⁶ "But you were not willing to go up. You rebelled against the command of the LORD your God. ²⁷ You grumbled in your tents and said, 'The LORD brought us out of the land of Egypt to hand us over to the Amorites in order to destroy us, because he hates us. ²⁸ Where can we go? Our brothers have made us lose heart, saying: The people are larger and taller than we are; the cities are large, fortified to the heavens. We also saw the descendants of the Anakim there.' ²⁹ "So I said to you: Don't be terrified or afraid of them!

[30] The LORD your God who goes before you will fight for you, just as you saw him do for you in Egypt. [31] And you saw in the wilderness how the LORD your God carried you as a man carries his son all along the way you traveled until you reached this place. [32] But in spite of this you did not trust the LORD your God."

In your own words, describe the Lord as He's revealed in this passage.

Why do you think the people doubted not just God's power but God's character? Do you relate to this? Explain.

In Egypt, their enemy was their oppressors. Who do they believe is their enemy now (v. 28)?

What is actually their enemy?

Deuteronomy means "second law" because it's Moses offering God's law to the new generation. When people forget God's words, home suffers greatly.

Where have you already seen evidence in Scripture of the danger of forgetting God's words?

Where have you seen evidence of that in your life?

LOOK UP DEUTERONOMY 30:19-20. **Why do you think Moses said this to the new generation?**

Their parents had not chosen God's ways and thus, not chosen life. (In fact, they'd gone even farther than treating God's goodness with suspicion; they suspected God was evil!) But this new generation had an opportunity to live differently as they stepped into this new home: rather than follow their fathers' ways, they could follow the Father's ways. If they loved the Lord—the Life-Giver—with their whole hearts, they would thrive in the land God provided.

LOOK UP ISAIAH 46:3-4.

Who is God talking to through the prophet Isaiah, and what is His promise to them?

What does this teach you about God's character?

Dear sister, your Keeper cares for and carries you. When you struggle to follow His word, cling to His character. He is compassionate and gracious, slow to anger and abounding in faithful love and truth. He is the Life-Giver whose way is life! Remember that though the story of home in Scripture zigs and zags, every angle points to God's faithfulness. This is true in your story, too.

DAY FOUR

The Home Where Promises Live

We know the bad home moments invite us to cling to God's promises of home, but the good home moments do, too. They are a glimmer of a better thing. The good things we've experienced are like movie previews, breadcrumbs, menu descriptions, neon arrows (pick your favorite metaphor) pointing us home.

FLIP OPEN YOUR BIBLE TO 1 KINGS 8, **which is probably the best "story of home" before Jesus.**

You could say it's the peak "home" moment of the Old Testament—a moment when God's people probably thought, "He did it! God did everything He said He would do. He is with us! We are home!"

Think about all that has led up to this moment in Scripture. God's people had spent years wandering in the wilderness, longing for the comforts of home. Then they'd spent years enjoying the comforts of home in the promised land. But unfortunately, they became numb to the Lord and dissatisfaction grew in their hearts. Sin was still the same enemy it was in the wilderness; it was just harder to spot in the land flowing with milk and honey. (Do you relate to this?)

But at this point of King Solomon's reign, things were swelling like a song leading up to the bridge, like a blueberry so ripe it's about to fall right off the bush. Abraham's descendants were a nation, had the promised land, were enjoying great blessings, and were blessing others around them. More than that, God was with them, and they knew it. In this chapter, we learn that King Solomon finally completed the temple, a "permanent" worship spot that functioned like an upgraded tabernacle. God's glory was more obvious to the people than ever!

Read the following passages to experience the excitement of this big moment.

VERSES 1-3,10-11

For what event are the people gathered?

When the priests came out of the holy place in the temple, what happened?

What does this passage teach you about God's glory?

VERSES 15-20

What had God promised David?

How was that promise fulfilled?

David desired to build a dwelling for God—but God told David that his son would do this instead. In this scene, David's son Solomon is dedicating the long-awaited dwelling place for the Lord! David didn't live to see this moment, but God always keeps His promises.

VERSES 27-30

What do you learn about God's limitlessness in this passage?

How did Solomon appeal to God as the Keeper, who keeps a watchful eye on His people?

What do you think it means for God's name to dwell in this place? What was Solomon asking of God? *(Hint: Remember Exodus 34:6b-7.)*

God's name is more than just a label—it represents who He is. This temple wouldn't just belong to the Lord; it would point to His character. It would help His people remember what He is like and worship Him as He actually is.

God's character is a big deal! Solomon knew God's name and knew what God is like, and this greatly informed his prayers. Similar to Moses, Solomon prayed by appealing to God's character.

What does it mean for the character of God to inform the way you pray?

How is that happening in your praying?

In verse 30, King Solomon prayed,

> Hear the petition of your servant
> and your people Israel,
> which they pray toward this place.
> May you hear in your dwelling place in heaven.
> May you hear and forgive.

For much of the rest of this chapter, Solomon elaborated on this idea. He presented different situations before the Lord (and in front of the people) of ways that God's people might sin or suffer. Yet, Solomon prayed, if they turn toward this temple and pray with wholehearted repentance, God please hear and forgive them!

What were some of the situations Solomon presented to the Lord? (I've filled in a few; you fill in the rest.)

VV. 31-32	If two people have a dispute about who has wronged whom
VV. 33-34	
VV. 35-36	
VV. 37-40	When there is famine, plague, disease, personal affliction
VV. 41-43	When a foreigner hears about God
VV. 44-45	
VV. 46-53	When God sends His people into enemy lands because of their sin

In all of these situations, Solomon asked the Lord to hear the praying person who would indicate their wholehearted devotion to God by praying toward the temple. This place was designed to be a prominent reminder of God's presence and a special opportunity for God to display His glory. When they looked toward the temple, God's people could remember His compassion and graciousness, His slowness to anger, His faithful love and respond with genuine worship. When they looked toward the temple, it was like waving at the promises of home, "greeting them from afar," like Hebrews 11:13 (ESV) says. God's people could remember that they were under the watchful gaze of their Keeper, the One who would never slumber or sleep (Ps. 121).

How do you see the temple pointing to Jesus?

Colossians 1:15 calls Jesus "the image of the invisible God" and then continues in verse 19 to say, "For God was pleased to have all his fullness dwell in him." Yes, the temple in Solomon's day was a place where God dwelled, but when Jesus came to live among us, He was the truer temple. All of God's character, all of His goodness, all of His glory was seen in Jesus.

LOOK UP 1 KINGS 9:3-9.

How did God answer Solomon's prayer?

What would happen if God's people allowed sin to make its home in their hearts?

How did God's response show He cares more about people's hearts than sacred buildings?

Throughout the Bible, we've seen that sin is the enemy of home—and God, as the Creator, Designer, Builder, Promiser, and Presence of home—defends home by battling against sin.

Tragically, the last scenario Solomon mentioned—God sending His people into enemy lands because of their sin—was a prophetic word. The nation of Israel divided after Solomon's reign. Then, king after king led the people to sin (though there were a few godly kings along the way), and as generation after generation failed to listen to God's warnings through His prophets, God did what He said He would do. God sent His people into exile.

The memorable, peak moment when God's people worshiped Him, when their leader prayed and honored God, when God's glory kept the priests from doing their work, perhaps even knocking them off their feet—it was just a temporary experience of home. God's people would look back and grieve. They were not home yet.

But although the worst was yet to come, so was the best. God would keep His promises.

DAY FIVE

Where Are You?

A big theme in this part of God's story of home is the importance of God's presence. It's a vital part of His promises. Home simply isn't home without Him.

This is a quotable concept, but it has roots. Think about the way God identified Himself to Moses. He said, "I AM WHO I AM." In all places, at all times, and in all circumstances, God is and God is who He is.

Consider that list of characteristics from Exodus 34:6b-7. If at this moment or any moment you long for someone to be compassionate to you, for someone to be gracious to you, for someone to be slow to anger, for someone to love you with a love that won't give up . . .

If at this moment or any moment, you have been hurt because someone didn't extend those attributes toward you or even showed you the opposite . . .

Who God is, is good news for you.

You can experience more of who He is exactly where you are if you will realize and acknowledge where you are and who He is. Often, paying attention to our soul's GPS allows us to more deeply understand God's promises and, in turn, walk in faith knowing that He will accomplish them. As Elizabeth Woodson says, "God's character shows us that His promises are true and will be fulfilled. The promises of God serve as a powerful lifeline during seasons of longing."[7]

I want to share with you a letter from a fellow sister in Christ. As she shares her story of home, I hope it'll point you to God's story of home and give you an opportunity to notice where you are—not home yet.

Dear Sister,

Have you ever needed to make a home in a place where nothing was familiar and all those who knew you best were far away? Have you gotten the chance to see God provide home for you even there? When I moved to Japan seven years ago, I spent a year and a half in the honeymoon of all that was new and bright and hoped for in this place God had called my family. Then, when I had my second baby, God allowed all of it to lose its luster, and I found myself deeply lonely and lost. The daily language school rhythm with its friendly interactions and clear expectations was now a thing of the past for me. I was in my house, jobless for the first time, with two kids and few friends. When I ventured outside my house, I was using a hopelessly floundering grasp on a new language to try and build connections with people who did not share my culture or history, had grown up with none of the same shows (except, hilariously, "Full House"), and believed none of the things I did about a Savior God and the world He made and loves.

It was during that time that God broke in and made a home for me even in this most unlikely place. Sister, I would love to tell you that this happened quickly, in a flash of heavenly intervention and all was well and right. But that is not the road God chose for me. I am assuming it is not for most of you either. I remember the place I was standing when I first realized that Moses was in Midian for forty years before God called him to deliver his fellow Israelites from their enslavers and another forty in the desert between Egypt and the promised land. I was so struck by the sheer amount of (seemingly) blank space in Moses's life.

The slow movements toward making a community and a home in Tokyo lasted through a year and a half of a colicky baby and an active toddler, months of a global pandemic and lock down, and hours upon hours of stilted conversations with the people God provided. However, as I look forward to the fifth birthday of my son, I can honestly tell you that God has made a home for me here. He has provided language skills, friendships, hobbies, and ministries. But most of all, He has provided Himself.

During my season of loneliness, I also walked through a season of doubt that had the twists and turns of its own story, but it brought me to my knees in a deep awe for the truth and majesty of a God who really did make me and really did burst into this world in a flash of heavenly intervention, writing Himself into the story of the world He made, to do what needed to be done to make His forever home with me—in this life, no matter where it takes me, and in the life to come. All the external things, like the waves from friends on the street as I go through my day, are gifts that display His delight in me; but that anchor—that home for my soul—is what holds me.

— **KATIE SAUNDERS**, missionary, Japan

Katie is my dear sister-in-law! We married brothers.

Use the space below (or your own journal) to respond to this letter. You may want to use the following questions to guide your response.

What thoughts and feelings are you experiencing as you consider this sister's story?

What from her letter most resonates with you and why?

How does her story help you understand God's story of home, reveal where you are, or help you find your way home to Him?

Going Home

Trapped in an unsafe home
Mistreated and hurt
God's people cried out
And their Keeper, He heard

Through all those years
Of longing for escape
It was finally time
God made a way

It started with a baby
In the water placed
A son surrendered
By another raised

He often felt alone
Cause the home he knows is
His enemy's home
You know him; it's Moses

He fled once in fear
And Pharaoh didn't lament him
But he returned, God with Him
He returned 'cause God sent him

God's people were freed
From external oppressors
But the enemy within
Kept them chained as transgressors

This kept them from home
This too was unsafe
God spoke, and they scoffed
Anti-God, anti-faith

So the promise was given
to the next generation
They would be the receivers
Of land, blessing, and nation

But even in the days
Of God's presence and temple
It was never that pure
It was never that simple

Sin kept winning
They rarely fought it
They heard sin's lies
They indulged it; they bought it

The worst is to come
Tempting us to despair
Why so easy to wander?
To believe God doesn't care?

No matter what comes
The Bible's clearly shown
God is still I AM
He will bring His people home

away from home

session four

By the rivers of Babylon—
there we sat down and wept
when we remembered Zion.

PSALM 137:1

God's people were finally home in the promised land, and you'd think it'd be smooth sailing—a "happily ever after" kind of situation. But they continuously welcomed the enemy of home—sin—into their hearts. God sent what seems like zillions of prophets to sound an alarm—like the kind that tells you when someone is breaking and entering. But God's people didn't care. They couldn't and wouldn't see sin as an enemy. So, God did what He said He would do: He sent physical enemies into the land to remove the people from their home. They went into exile. Far away from all that was familiar, God's people had to grapple with the physical evidence of what had been spiritually true for a long while: they were not at home with God.

VIEWER GUIDE

session four

Watch the Session Four video. Use this page to take notes, capture quotes, or doodle some thoughts from the video teaching session.

To access the video teaching sessions, use the instructions in the back of your Bible study book.

DISCUSSION/REFLECTION QUESTIONS

If you're doing this study with a group, be ready to discuss these questions during your time together. (If you're leading a group, check out the leader guide at lifeway.com/comehome to help you prepare.) If you're doing this study solo, use the following questions to reflect on what you've heard in the video teaching.

1   What is one thing in the video teaching that stood out to you? Why?

2   When was a time you were the most homesick?

3   Do you think God treated the people of Israel too harshly with the exile? Explain.

4   In those times when sin was having its way in your life, how did God get your attention and call you back to Him?

5   What are your thoughts and feelings about Psalm 137, especially verses 8-9? Can you understand the sentiment? Can you learn from it? Explain.

6   How would you define lament? Do you feel freedom to express your hurt, pain, and even your anger and hate to the Lord? If not, what's hindering you from being able to lament?

7   What strikes you the most about Daniel's prayer in Daniel 6:10—his posture, his direction, his words, his discipline? How should his prayer shape your own prayer life?

8   If someone asked you what you learned in our time together today, what would you say?

DAY ONE

God's Presence—Gone

As we talked about in our teaching session, when Ezekiel was situated far from Jerusalem at the Chebar canal in Babylon, he saw a vision of God's glory leaving the temple (Ezek. 10–12).

This was significant, because even while in exile, God's people struggled to believe that the exile events were from God's hand. Even though their sin was so blatant, they struggled to see it—or more likely, they wouldn't see it. They weren't willing to even imagine they were sinners who deserved judgment.

Have you ever had a season in which you were willfully blind to your sin? If so, describe it.

In what kind of situations do you think people are most prone to be numb to God's Word?

In a sin-sick world, where sensitivity to sin continues to fade, it can be challenging to view sin as a big deal, and it can be even more challenging to confront our own sin. Why is it important for us to understand and acknowledge that we've sinned?

What made matters worse for the people of God was that many false prophets pretended to have heard from God and told the people exactly what they wanted to hear.

LOOK UP JEREMIAH 23:16-32.

What message were the false prophets spreading, and why would it be a popular one?

What message did God actually send through His true prophets (v. 22)?

How does this passage reveal that God Himself brought about the exile?

What does this passage say about God's character? How does that resonate with you?

God's people wanted peace without the God of peace. God's people wanted peace while making war against God with their sin. The false prophets gave them permission to live this way with their misleading message. The people invested in this godless thinking to their own demise.

Of course, God is I AM. He knew what would happen, and He'd been warning them for years and years. The book of Deuteronomy bears witness to this. As we stated last week, Deuteronomy is the second telling of God's law, offered by Moses to the new generation who was about to enter the promised land. Ironically, the wonderfulness of the promised land left God's people uniquely vulnerable to sin. Even in "perfect" homes, sin has a way of sneaking in. When things are going exceedingly well for us, we can't drop our guard against sin.

READ DEUTERONOMY 8:11-20.

Why do you think we are prone to forget God when life is full?

How can you be on guard against sin during this season? How can you enjoy God's blessings without forgetting "Every good and perfect gift is from above, coming down from the Father of lights" (Jas. 1:17)?

Later in Deuteronomy, God warned Moses about the people's future rebellion (31:15-17). In Deuteronomy 32, God wrote a song through Moses to bear witness to their disobedience, so they would know that their "many troubles and afflictions" were a result of their sinful actions. And perhaps, the song which would be passed down to their descendants, would lead future generations to repentance. God's people would carry God's melody in their vocal cords to remember what was true.

Though much of the tune is a song of betrayal, God promises vindication and compassion for His people in the end (vv. 36-43). The fact that God packaged His promises with a song reveals His wisdom and care. We may be prone to forget things, but songs have a way of sticking with us no matter what. Have you ever heard a song from decades ago and somehow you know every word? Or how a person suffering from a disease like Alzheimer's might forget the names of their loved ones but can still recognize a beloved hymn?

Moses sang this song over the people as some of his last words, the grand finale of the "retelling of the law." This is how he concluded:

> 45 When Moses finished reciting all these words to all Israel, 46 he said to them, "Take to heart all the words I have solemnly declared to you this day, so that you may command your children to obey carefully all the words of this law. 47 They are not just idle words for you—they are your life. By them you will live long in the land you are crossing the Jordan to possess."
>
> DEUTERONOMY 32:45-47 (NIV)

How did Moses describe God's words in these verses?

What promise from God was connected to their obedience to His words?

Why is it dangerous to cling to God's promises while forgetting God's instructions?

Unfortunately, even though they were armed with Moses's song and even though God faithfully sent prophets to reorient them to the truth, God's people did what He said they would do. They forgot Him. They were full from the blessings of the promised land, and it numbed them to see what truly made the promised land significant: the God who gave the blessings.

And so, God left.

Of course, even though God's presence left the temple, He was still I AM. That means no matter what, no matter when, no matter where, He Is. And yet, He removed this special expression of His presence from the sacred place so that His people could remember that His presence is the truest gift, the ultimate welcome mat, that which makes home *home*. Without God's presence, God's promises lose their glory! He was training His people to want Him—not just what He could give them. After all, the whole aim of His story of home is for God and His people to dwell together!

Why do you think we're prone to want God's promises without God's presence? How has that been evidenced in your life?

As it turns out, home was more than a place, more than people, more than peace; it was a Person. Without God's glory, home was no home.

And yet there is good news ahead.

Yes, Ezekiel testified to the removal of God's glory, but that's not the end of the story.

LOOK UP JOHN 17:24 **and write below what Jesus prayed.**

DAY TWO

Lamenting with Psalm 137:1-7

Listen up. It's time to look at Psalm 137. Gird your loins.

For a preview of today's study, make sure you've watched the Session Four teaching video.

If you've already watched it, what stood out to you and what questions do you have?

READ PSALM 137. **To help you pay attention to the text, you may want to (1) double underline any locations and (2) draw a box around any mentions of people or people groups.**

VERSE 1

The psalmist was preserving a memory of homesickness.

Where is he, and where does he long to be?

Zion represents their homeland, both the land and the temple.

Rivers is significant, too. If you remember, Ezekiel and the exiles with him were at the Chebar canal, a waterway that flowed southeast from the city of Babylon.[1] There are two likely reasons why the psalmist was with other exiles near a river: (1) Work. The exiles were likely forced to build and maintain irrigation ditches for the Babylonian empire.[2] (2) Worship. The nearness to water was helpful for ritual washing or waterside locations may have been easy gathering places. (See Acts 16:13.)

The time together by the waters of Babylon moved the exiles to remember home—and to weep for what had been lost.

VERSES 2-4

The captives hung their lyres on the poplar trees.

How might this have been an act of mourning or protest?

A lyre is a stringed instrument that was often used to accompany songs of praise and celebration. However, this was not a time of celebration but of heartache. Thus, the captives had no need of them.

The request to sing was cruel. The tormentors knew their captives' music was sacred, linked to deep memories of the land and temple they destroyed. As we noted yesterday, music is powerful. It is somewhat of a teleportation device.

What familiar song transports you back to a different time or place?

A song about home can be painful when we are in a distant land. And these weren't just any songs, but "the LORD's songs." Powerfully, he used God's divine name as a descriptor—the name that reveals God's character (Ex. 34:6-7), was placed on the temple (1 Kings 9:3), and implies limitlessness.[3] Perhaps this name was somewhat of an anchor for a limited and lamenting man.

VERSES 5-6

The psalmist committed to remembering Jerusalem. Not just the holy city, but the holy God the city represented.

READ DEUTERONOMY 8:11-14. **What did God's people need to be careful not to do?**

How might Psalm 137:5-6 be words of repentance?

God's people were in exile for not remembering God and His words, for not worshiping wholeheartedly, for finding their joy in idols rather than in worshiping the true God. The psalmist was saying, "If I forget you, may I cease to make music forever." In other words, what use is music without the Person and the place who inspired it?

VERSE 7

At this point we begin to sense not just sadness from the psalmist—but deep anger. Perhaps that's why we feel uncomfortable.

It helps to understand why he was so angry. The Edomites were neighbors to God's people. When enemies came to conquer Jerusalem, the Edomites cheered. They rooted for the sacred city to fall.

Has someone ever seen you in pain and cheered? If so, how did that feel?

The Edomites were descendants of Esau (Gen. 25:30; 36:9). What do you remember about "Edom's" relationship with Israel (Jacob)?

Jacob and Esau had a rocky and sometimes murderous relationship. The way sin lures people who are family to turn against one another is a dark theme in Scripture. It started with Cain and Abel, continued with Jacob and Esau, and is also seen in the relationship among Jacob's sons (Joseph and his brothers).

Perhaps the psalmist saw the exile as a sort of large-scale version of brotherly betrayal. Something in him screamed, "It shouldn't be this way!" He wanted God to remember the depth of betrayal and how their enemies desired for their precious home to be destroyed.

But the Hebrew word *remember* is more that just "recall." It implies action.[4] The psalmist wanted God to see and to do something about this injustice.

Are you familiar with this desire? Explain.

Early on in our ministry career, my pastor husband and I were deeply betrayed in a way that meant we had to leave our home. It wasn't exile, but it felt like exile. Every box I packed testified to our mistreatment. The "family" that we thought loved us suddenly viewed us as enemies. Though there were public smiles, behind closed doors some people rooted for and even plotted our suffering.

I remember sitting in my daughter's nursery, overcome with affection for this precious room and all the memories it held, weeping as I peeled off the gold polka dots that I'd so happily placed on the walls in anticipation of her arrival. How had our beloved home been taken from us so quickly? I was deeply saddened and deeply angered.

Have you had a similar painful "home" experience? Explain.

In case you are in a situation like this, I want to carefully remind you that forgiveness doesn't always mean a restoration of trust or a need to reestablish the relationship. With God's help, I am able to forgive (and keep forgiving) the people who harmed us while also wisely knowing that I should not entrust my family to them. This goes beyond the scope of this study, but if you desire help in this area, consider meeting with a trusted and godly friend, pastor, or biblical counselor.

Many years have passed since that time, and I no longer yearn for that home. In fact, I am now utterly convinced that this painful experience was God's mercy to my family. (Thank you, God! Seriously, thank you, God.)

Even still, pain from that season surfaces from time to time. A counselor advised me to surrender to God's sight. She said, "He sees this, and He sees that it was wrong." She also advised me to surrender to God's justice. Because God "remembers"—sees in a way that implies action—I can trust Him to act on my behalf and can commit to a posture of forgiveness toward those who harmed us.

As pastor and podcaster Paul Carter says in an immensely helpful article about Psalm 137, "In the end, no one gets away with anything. All sins will be paid for in blood. Either the blood of Christ or the blood of sinners. It is not wrong to long for the justice of God."[5]

Friend, God remembers the painful parts of your story. Through Him justice is yours, "either the blood of Christ or the blood of sinners." Sin is always a big deal to God, and He will always address it.

It might feel wrong for the psalmist to want God to see and to do something about this injustice, but it isn't. The psalmist wasn't taking vengeance into his own hands; his cry was "Remember, LORD!"

> **Is there an event in your "story of home" you need to surrender to God's sight and justice? If so, write your own version of verse 7 in the space below.**

Sin is the enemy of home, but God promises justice. As we look to Him for our true home, we are not out of bounds to look to Him for justice. As we do, we can forgive others, empowered by the forgiveness we have in Him.

DAY THREE

Lamenting with Psalm 137:8-9

Today we're getting back into Psalm 137—and getting into the most uncomfortable part, verses 8-9. In the words of Steven Curtis Chapman, "Saddle up your horses. We've got a trail to blaze."

Full disclosure: I've fallen off every horse I've ever gotten on, except for Old Maid, the horse I rode at a friend's birthday party when I was ten. She was specifically chosen for me to ride because they said she was too gentle and old to knock me off. Unfortunately, Old Maid got lost in the woods, with me on her back, sobbing in a denim hat with attached sunflower. Studying Psalm 137 may feel a little like that at times, but we will eventually find our way back to the birthday party.

> *REREAD PSALM 137* **and glance over your notes from yesterday's study. Once you're reacquainted with Psalm 137, meet me back here.**

VERSES 8-9

Armed with a deeper understanding of verse 7, it's easier to see that verses 8-9 are words of confidence in God. The psalmist knows God is a God of justice, and God will bring justice. (Because we are on this side of the cross, we understand that the blood of Jesus offers justice for sin while providing rescue for sinners.)

> **Pick two or three of the following verses to read: Deuteronomy 32:35; 1 Samuel 24:12; Psalm 94:1; Romans 12:19; Hebrews 10:30. What do these verses say about God?**

> **Do you ever want to make your own justice? What's a biblical response to that impulse?**

Even when we understand that the psalmist is looking to God for justice rather than seeking to create his own justice, there are two sticky places we need to talk about in verses 8-9.

1. First, the word "happy" or "blessed." Eek.

The most common translations of the Bible use the words *happy* or *blessed* in verses 8-9. It's fair to say we are not happy about nor feeling particularly blessed by this particular word being used in this particular place. *Happy* is a word we prefer being written on a cake in front of the word *birthday*, you know?

But we are a part of a specific culture during a specific time, and words are funny little creatures that change clothes depending on the setting. (Case in point: Your granddaddy might have worn a "cap" but your Gen Z neighbor uses this word to talk about lying. "No cap.") This word usage problem is made more complicated because the Old Testament was written in Hebrew, a language known for having meaning-rich words.[6] Thus *happy* or *blessed* in verses 8-9 has more depth than we of the "Happy Birthday" and "#blessed" culture might initially understand.

The Hebrew word *esher* used here and typically translated *blessed* is taken from the root word *ashar*, which means "to go straight, go on, advance." So "blessedness" or "happiness" is not a flippant or light "happy birthday" but something more substantial that stems from doing the right thing. Look at some other places the root word is used:

- "Listen, my son, and be wise; *keep* your mind on the right course." (Prov. 23:19)

- "Learn to do what is good. Pursue justice. *Correct* the oppressor." (Isa. 1:17a)

With this in mind, how might the word translated *blessed* or *happy* be a justice word?

Scholar J. Alec Motyer translated the word like this in verse 9: "How right he will be who seizes and shatters your children against a rock!"[7] The psalmist believes it will be just, right, and fair if God repays Babylon "with what you have done to us." And what has Babylon done to the exiles? This helps us deal with the second bit of sticky business.

2. Second, the dashing of babies on rocks. Double eek. Triple eek. All the eeks!

This part makes us the most uncomfortable, understandably. We are right to be shocked by this. It makes sense that this passage is famously avoided.

But when we pay close attention to verse 8 "happy is the one who pays you back what you have done to us," we realize that verse 9 reveals what Babylon had already done to the exiles. Babylon had dashed *their* children against the rocks. The psalmist was not inventing a dark punishment for his oppressors; he was preserving a horrific, traumatic memory. He was asking God to give them justice for what had been brutally done to them.

> **How does it change your understanding of the psalm to realize the psalmist is recalling something that had already happened?**

> **Does the psalmist now seem blood-thirsty or justice-seeking? Explain.**

> **How does this memory increase the cruelty of the captors asking them to sing?**

The horrific killing of little ones is something we see elsewhere in Scripture.

> *READ EXODUS 1:8-10,22 AND MATTHEW 2:16-18.* **In each instance, who is under attack? Who is attacking? Why?**

By God's design, both Moses and Jesus—deliverers the rulers feared—were spared by supernatural means.

Jesus and Moses were both spared for specific purposes, but Jesus's purpose carried eternal significance for all people. In God's design and timing, He came to live a perfect life and die a punishing, but atoning death at the hands of betrayers and oppressors.

Consider all the ways this psalm points to Jesus:

- God the Father allowed His own Son—His little one—to be dashed.[8]

- God the Son willingly hung on a tree, like those lyres on the poplars, as many of His followers sat down and wept.[9]

- Just as the exiles were mocked by their tormentors, "Sing us one of the songs of Zion," God the Son was mocked, too. "He saved others; let him save himself" (Luke 23:35-39).

Psalm 137 is a difficult lament, designed to help God's people through difficult times.

The psalmist asked the question, "How can we sing the Lord's song on foreign soil?" How might we also sing Psalm 137? How can this song be a help to us?

This song is an enduring one. It reverberates in our hearts as we suffer the horrors of the world. It is not our home. Our trials aren't the same as exile, but they can feel like exile.

This text provides us the opportunity to pray our hate, to pray our anger, to pray our mistreatment to a God who sees, who will act on our behalf, and who did not spare His own "little one" from the hands of betrayers and oppressors so that all who look to Him might have salvation. When we view it with the gospel in mind, we remember that not only is our pain seen, it is understood. Jesus understands our stories, and He will not only show us the way home, He will carry us there.

DAY FOUR

Praying God's Promises

During the exile, Daniel was a man who kept his eyes toward home and Home Maker, despite how Babylonian leaders sought to strip him of his heritage. He's a powerful example of faithfulness to God in the midst of a foreign land. While he was estranged, he was willing to be strange. He prayed on a regular basis, obeyed God's laws, and read God's Word.

In this time of great despair, God's Word, through Jeremiah, provided Daniel with profound hope.

LOOK UP JEREMIAH 25:11-13 AND JEREMIAH 29:10 **to see some of what Daniel read. What do these two passages say about the exile?**

When Daniel realized the exile had an expiration date that was quickly approaching, he responded in a very Daniel way. He prayed.

READ DANIEL 9:1-19.

Describe Daniel's posture as he prayed (v. 3).

According to Daniel, why were the exiles in exile?

According to Daniel, why should God deliver them?

How can you tell that Daniel desired God's presence and not merely stuff or events God had promised?

Daniel was saturated with God's Word! In this text, he referenced both Jeremiah and Moses. In mentioning Moses, Daniel was speaking of the first five books of the Old Testament. He also listed characteristics of God over and over again. This was a man who truly sought to know God as He has revealed Himself in His Word! As a result, Daniel also had a clear and accurate understanding of his people and their sin. (When we look at God, it's easier to see our sin.)

How did Daniel describe his people and his God in each of the following verses?

Verses 4-6

Verse 7

Verses 8-9

Verse 14

Verse 15

Sometimes when we want someone to get over something we've done, we downplay it and act like it wasn't that bad. Daniel did the exact opposite. He desired God's mercy, so he was brutally honest about the shortcomings of his people and appealed to God's character. In other words, Daniel wasn't saying, "What we've done isn't that bad." He was saying, "Who You are is so good!"

What do you learn from Daniel's prayer that should shape your prayer life?

Interestingly, Daniel lived righteously, yet aligned himself with his deeply sinful people and sought God's favor on their behalf. How does this point us to Jesus?

Sometimes we feel like we "ought" to read God's Word and pray, but how might Daniel's example stir up in us a genuine desire to do those things?

READ DANIEL 9:21-23 to see what happened as a result of Daniel's prayer.

When did Gabriel leave to meet Daniel? What does this reveal about God?

Daniel didn't ask for understanding, but God wanted to give it to him anyway! According to the text, why did God want to do this?

Gabriel went on to share a mysterious and number-laden prophecy, which you can read in Daniel 9:24-27 if you like. On one hand, the prophecy was bad news—the seventy years was just the start of their waiting. The coming "home going" wouldn't truly feel like home. (The books of Ezra and Nehemiah give evidence that this was true.) Sin was the true enemy that needed to be dealt with, not the Babylonians. Sin was still at home in people's hearts and still needed to be destroyed.

God's people longed to go back home (and technically they would), but in the fullness of time, a truer home would be revealed. God would "bring the rebellion to an end," "put a stop to sin," "atone for iniquity," "bring in everlasting righteousness," "seal up vision and prophecy," and "anoint the most holy place" (all phrases from verse 24). How would He do this? How would He deal with the enemy of sin and make the way home? With the coming of the "Anointed One" (v. 25). The Greek word *Christ* and the Hebrew word

Messiah both mean "Anointed One." Most commentators believe in one way or another, this mysterious, number-laden prophecy points to Jesus!

As I'm sure you can imagine, there has been much discussion about the numbers found in verses 24-27. When we encounter a number in the Bible, our tendency is to think like a math student, but we should also think like a literature student. Numbers are deeply symbolic!

The Daniel text mainly features sevens. In ancient near eastern and Israelite culture, seven represented fullness or completeness. (In fact, the Hebrew word for seven is spelled with the same consonants as the word that means complete/full.[10]) For example, think about how God created the world and rested on the seventh day, as if enjoying its completeness. Daniel had been amazed by God's promise to Jeremiah to complete the exile in seven decades, but as David Guzik says, "It was as if God said through Gabriel, 'Now I will show you some 'sevens' that will really amaze you.'"[11] Gabriel spoke of what would happen in "seventy sevens"—the ultimate mark of completion.

> *READ THE FOLLOWING TRANSLATIONS OF GALATIANS 4:4-5* **and circle the part about completion/fullness of time.**
>
> - ESV: But when the fullness of time had come, God sent forth his Son, born of woman, born under the law, to redeem those who were under the law, so that we might receive adoption as sons.
>
> - CSB: When the time came to completion, God sent his Son, born of a woman, born under the law, to redeem those under the law, so that we might receive adoption as sons.
>
> **What happened in the "fullness of time"?**

Out of deep affection for Daniel, God the Father spilled the beans (albeit, mysterious beans) about His plan to send God the Son to make the way home by defeating the enemy of sin and making a way for God and people to be together. This is a much better promise of home than return from exile. Jesus is the only One who would be able to fulfill the Exile promise: "I will give you new hearts, and I will bring you home."

> **How can Daniel's prayer and God's answer encourage us as we navigate seasons that feel like exile?**

DAY FIVE

Where Are You?

The exile reminds us that mistreatment, betrayal, anger, hate, and horror might feel like unwanted, unfair, and unexpected plot twists in our stories of home—but these actions and emotions are the results when sin is wreaking havoc.

Whether you have endured these things because of your own sin, because of the direct sin of another, or because you simply live in a world impacted by sin, you can know that God the Father remembers what you've endured (meaning He sees and will act!) and God the Son understands what you've endured.

I want to share with you a letter from a fellow sister in Christ. As she shares her story of home, I hope it'll point you to God's story of home and give you an opportunity to notice where you are—not home yet.

Dear Sister,

I once imagined home as a beautifully decorated house filled with necessities and sentimental items—fruit and family photos. Throughout my childhood, I lived the complete opposite. My place was anything but ideal. Anger, danger, fear, and sorrow settled in my living room. The space felt more like a house inhabited by wounded souls. Born in a dysfunctional home and hurt by broken people, I wished for better.

One day, I walked a winding Mississippi road littered with crunchy leaves while breathing in the autumn air. "What am I doing?" I asked myself. My legs had carried me out of my traumatic environment. I didn't know it, but I would enter a domestic abuse shelter later that evening. A place that terrified me would be described as a "temporary home." It would be a safe place with provision, helpful people, and rest. Tears would overfill my eyes when repeating the phrase "temporary home." It was both painful and relieving; I questioned, "Where is my forever home?"

By the grace of God, I was adopted into a family with sentimental photos, my face in several frames, and I freely grabbed bananas from the bowl of fruit on the counter. I had a God-fearing father who I knew would always protect and lead us. A mother whose love felt like ointment. Laughter, prayer, Bibles, and hugs filled the rooms. There, I received everything I had longed for in a home.

Each place taught me that earthly dwellings can yield both brokenness and beauty. But God with us is home here on earth and is a taste of the fullness to come. The most beautiful, comfortable home is flawed. We are all prone to sin and are in the hard and holy process of becoming more like Jesus. We journey through seasons of bliss and hardship. Yet, the God of hope walks us through every season.

The hoped-for home I desired in my youth changed with life's transitions. It became a college dorm, a shared house with roommates, a small upstairs room on a ranch, an even tinier room in a camper, and a cozy place with lots of space: many moves, yet God was with me.

Are you encountering the most overwhelming hardships of your life? Do you wonder why God would allow it? Are you unable to see the big story? God with you is home for now. Rest in this as you look forward to the glory of heaven. That home will have no sin, pain, sorrow, or trial.

Have you been blessed to experience the ideal home? Remember, there is much more. Let the gifts God has given you now point you to the delight of your eternal home.

continued →

May the trials and beauty of living the earthly experience lead you to the perfection of the new heavens and earth.

Where God is, there is home.

— JOSEPHINE D. ROSE, *writer, Mississippi*

Josephine lives near me and is one of my favorite people to get coffee with!

Use the space below (or your own journal) to respond to this letter. You may want to use the following questions to guide your response.

What thoughts and feelings are you experiencing as you consider this sister's story?

What from her letter most resonates with you and why?

How does her story help you understand God's story of home, reveal where you are, or help you find your way home to Him?

Away From Home

Deaf to the sirens,
The words of the prophets,
God's people were captured
Just as He promised

Their home was destroyed
Homesickness their story
They'd welcomed sin,
they'd exchanged glory

Exile brought pain
Separation from God the worst
If God promised blessings
Why did they feel cursed?

Lament was their song
Weeping their standard
But with eyes on God
They endured the slander

Praying with eyes toward home
God's character in mind
They knew He was I AM
In every place and time

Even away from home
They remained in God's view
He wouldn't delete the bad
But He would bring them through

They'd remake their home
But the very best part
Was the God-made change
He'd remake their hearts

Even away from home
God's mercies were new
God never changes
His promises still true

the way
home

session five

"Lord," Thomas said,
"we don't know where you're going.
 How can we know the way?"
Jesus told him, "I am the way . . . "

JOHN 14:5-6A

God's people finally returned home, but even this wasn't the great
homecoming they'd envisioned. Something wasn't quite right. The
prophet Ezekiel had told God's people they needed new hearts—
hearts that could and would follow God. But how could that
happen? Things seemed bleak and beige, but all the while God was
carrying out His plan. At just the right time, God the Father said
to His Son, "It's time to build the way home." God Himself came
to dwell on earth as a baby. As He grew, He pointed people to the
way. The way wasn't a path; it was a Person. It was Him. Jesus is the
answer to every promise of home that God has uttered along the
way, and through Him, all are invited: "Come home."

VIEWER GUIDE

session five

Watch the Session Five video. Use this page to take notes, capture quotes, or doodle some thoughts from the video teaching session.

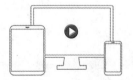

To access the video teaching sessions, use the instructions in the back of your Bible study book.

DISCUSSION/REFLECTION QUESTIONS

If you're doing this study with a group, be ready to discuss these questions during your time together. (If you're leading a group, check out the leader guide at lifeway.com/comehome to help you prepare.) If you're doing this study solo, use the following questions to reflect on what you've heard in the video teaching.

1   What is one thing in the video teaching that stood out to you? Why?

2   Ever been through a time when it felt like God was silent? Explain.

3   How does the genealogy in Matthew show us God was working out His plan the whole time? When you look back over your life history and beyond, how do you see God at work?

4   Does it seem absurd to you that the people of Jesus's day missed that He was the Messiah? How could that be? How do people today miss who Jesus is and their need for Him?

5   How is Jesus the fulfillment of Genesis 3:15?

6   How would you explain to someone who is not a Christian that Jesus is only the way home?

7   How has death been a cruel and terrifying enemy of home for you? How has Jesus given hope in this darkness?

8   If someone asked you what you learned in our time together today, what would you say?

DAY ONE

Jesus's Story of Home

Strangely enough, Jesus—the Way home—had a unique relationship with home from the very beginning of His earthly life. Jesus's personal experiences offer tender ministry to us. Consider what the author of Hebrews said about Jesus:

> For we do not have a high priest who is unable to sympathize with our weaknesses, but one who has been tempted in every way as we are, yet without sin.
>
> HEBREWS 4:15

The word translated *sympathize* means "to be affected with the same feeling as another."[1] Our world often equates power with the ability to remain unbothered. Yet, we have a Savior who has been willingly affected by the same weaknesses that affect us—and remained without sin. We do not have an aloof Savior—we have an affected One. In Jesus, we find both triumph and in-the-trenches tenderness. Praise God!

In short, Jesus understands the pains, joys, difficulties, and anxieties of your story of home—not just because He's God but because He's man and has experienced these things Himself.

Let's take a look at His earthly life.

BIRTH AND EARLY CHILDHOOD

Famously, Jesus's mother wasn't in her hometown of Nazareth when she gave birth to Him but in Bethlehem, where Mary and Joseph had traveled to be counted for a census. About 90 to 120 miles from home (depending on the route[2]), Mary and Joseph weren't able to secure lodging one could typically expect to find in first century Palestine. So, Mary gave birth in an environment that probably felt foreign to her in every way.

LOOK UP LUKE 1:30-33; 2:6-7.

How does this announcement about Jesus's birth differ from the conditions of Jesus's birth?

LOOK UP MATTHEW 2:13-23.

What part of this text . . .

    . . . reminds you of Moses's story as a baby?

    . . . reminds you of the Israelites' deliverance from Pharaoh?

    . . . reminds you of the exile?

How might the memory of the announcement about Jesus's birth (Luke 1:30-33) been a comfort to Mary and Joseph during this scary season?

How do you see God at work even in the upheaval?

Of course, Joseph, Mary, and Jesus's sudden refugee status wasn't sudden to God the Father. In fact, "God had prepared in advance for their needs: the expensive gifts from the magoi would have likely provided sufficient means for them to start over in a foreign country."[3]

ADOLESCENCE

READ LUKE 2:41-52.

While returning to Nazareth from the Passover festival in Jerusalem, Joseph and Mary discovered Jesus was not with them. They went back and found Him conversing with the teachers in the temple. This passage contains the first recorded words of Jesus.

What were His first words, and why were they significant?

Mary and Joseph were understandably rattled that Jesus was not with His family. Why do you think Jesus didn't seem rattled at all?

In this culture, it was normal for a son to take up his father's line of work, and since Jesus was twelve, He was near the time when sons began to be viewed as adults. Likely young Jesus was growing in His understanding of His relationship with God the Father and the ultimate work set before Him. But at this point, the time of His ministry was still years away. So, He went home with Mary and Joseph, was obedient to them, and grew in every way (Luke 2:51-52).

ADULTHOOD

LOOK UP JOHN 1:45-46. Nathanael's response to Philip could have been prompted by his remembering the prophecy that the Messiah would be born in Bethlehem, not Nazareth. Or, he could have been revealing how people felt about Nazareth.

If the latter, what does that say about the reputation of Jesus's hometown?

LOOK UP LUKE 9:57-58.

Throughout Jesus's ministry, we see Him stay in the homes of others, but He did not have a home of His own. When He wanted to retreat from the world (and He often did!), He would slip away to a quiet, outdoor place and pray.

What did Jesus say about His home in this passage?

Jesus said this in response to someone who promised to follow Jesus "wherever" He went. Why do you think Jesus responded in a way that seems on the surface to be so discouraging?

READ MARK 3:21 AND JOHN 7:5.

As we've said many times, home is not merely a place. Our families have such an impact on our stories of home. What family tension do you see here?

Of course, the biblical authors only provide us with the tiniest glimpse into the experiences Jesus had in His earthly life. So much of the Gospels are about His teachings and His miracles. But as Hebrews tells us, Jesus "has been tempted *in every way* as we are" (emphasis added). If you have been displaced from your home, rejected by family, dismissed because of your background, or experienced that vague sense of "this is not my home" even while you're at home, Jesus understands this and any other painful home experience you've endured.

Use the space below to write a prayer both thanking Jesus for understanding you and asking Him to help you more deeply experience the blessing of being understood by Him.

DAY TWO

Jesus and the Temple

My brother has a close longtime friend named Michael Dean. One of the reasons we love him is because he's loud and ridiculous. (Michael Dean is one of those guys we always call by his full name. Notably, he has been known to bear false witness that his name is "Michelangelo Dean." He may have even had his name printed that way in a friend's wedding program, with the bride blissfully unaware that she'd printed Michael Dean's nod to the Ninja Turtles.) When the boys were in high school, Michael Dean came over to our house all the time. And there was one thing that always made him flip out: when Mom rearranged the furniture. "What is this?!" he would scream with his trademark pretend outrage.

Michael Dean's indignance would make sense if my mom went to *his* house and rearranged *his* furniture. But of course, when a place is yours, you get to move the furniture around as you see fit, no matter how much your son's friend screams about it. Mom has the authority to change where the couch is, and there's nothing Michael or Michelangelo Dean or the Ninja Turtles can do about it.

Here's where I'm going with this: The Gospel writers relate how Jesus entered the temple, created a whip, began to turn over tables, and seemingly flipped out. Jesus was well within His rights to do this because the temple was *His* house. In John 2:16, Jesus said, "Stop turning my Father's house into a marketplace!" Similarly, Jesus's time in the temple as a twelve-year-old boy helps us see that He cared deeply for this place, considered it His Father's house, and desired to be there (Luke 2:41-50). This was His Father's house—and therefore His house—and those in the temple had put everything in the wrong place.

READ MATTHEW 21:8-13.

> **As Jesus passed by, the people were shouting "Hosanna!" which originally meant "God save us!"[4] Have you had a "Hosanna!" moment in your life or a season in which you realized your need for a Savior? Describe it.**

What did Jesus find when He entered the temple?

What actions did He take in response to what He found?

The temple trained God's people to come to God in a particular place (the God-made meeting place) and a particular way (through sin-acknowledging sacrifice). Because Jews needed to travel from all over, it makes sense that they could and would purchase sacrificial animals on site rather than bring them along on the trip. (Try traveling long distances with a blemish-free lamb in tow and see if the little guy stays blemish-free!) However, they'd come to do business in the place that was designed for prayer! There was no need for these transactions to take place inside the temple. Plus, we can be sure there was some corruption involved—animals sold and money exchanged at outrageous prices. The Jewish leaders were providing a service while they lined their pockets.[5] Their actions might have appeared religious, but the set up was actually getting in the way of genuine worship of and connection with God.[6]

> **In your life, what gets in the way of praying and worshiping God, maybe even some things that might appear good or religious?**

I've often noticed salvation poetically described as Jesus making a heart His home. Interestingly, Tim Keller says after a genuine "Hosanna!" moment (salvation), Jesus comes in and "rearranges the furniture" of this home, much like He did during that temple cleansing.[7] When we welcome Jesus into our lives, we welcome whatever changes He wants to make in His house. Sometimes these changes are obvious—He helps thieves stop stealing and liars stop lying. But other changes are more subtle. There may be good things in our lives (a career, our kids, a spouse, a goal, a friend, etc.) that we have made to be "God things." There may also be things in our lives that appear religious (serving excessively at church, attending every Bible study, praying publicly with lots of flourish) but they are actually getting in the way of our genuine worship of and connection with God.

Are there any good things in your life that you've made into God things? If so, name them and describe how they are affecting your genuine worship of God and your connection to Him.

You can read about Jesus "cleansing" the temple in all the gospels: Matthew 21:12-13; Mark 11:15-17; Luke 19:45-46; and John 2:13-25. Some scholars debate if Jesus cleansed the temple once or twice, since John's account seems to place this event at the beginning of Jesus's ministry. However, some believe John simply changed the chronology of the event for theological reasons.

In 1 Corinthians 3:16, Paul stated that we, as the church, are God's temple and the Holy Spirit lives in us. (More on this next session!) Jesus had every right to rearrange the temple building—and every right to rearrange the hearts of temple believers because this is His house! But Jesus is more than just the true owner of the temple. He is the true temple!

READ JOHN 2:13-22.

What temple was Jesus speaking about in verse 19?

In your own words, explain what Jesus meant by this.

The Bible Project has an incredible video that shows how the temple is an important theme throughout Scripture, with the person of Jesus as the great hinge point.[8] Here's how I'd sum it up:

The world as it was originally designed (meaning creation pre-sin, including the garden in Eden), the tabernacle, and the temple, were all "temples" of sorts—places that overlap with God's heavenly home. God made these "homes" with care and intention where He could be together with His people. His ultimate goal for these homes was His glory, and humanity had a God-given purpose within these homes. When Adam and Eve sinned, attempting to rule apart from God, they were exiled from their home in Eden. This same thing happened when Israel's leaders attempted to rule apart from God. After the exile, the prophets spoke of a new temple and priesthood that would allow God's presence to fill all of creation (Hab. 2:14). Enter Jesus, who claimed to be the new temple—and claimed after His resurrection that God would come to dwell within His followers, making them temples. (More on this in the next teaching session!) Moreover, when Jesus returns, He will make all things new and wonderful and in this new creation God will dwell with His people. (More on this is coming up, too!)

LOOK UP MATTHEW 12:6. **Based on the temple overview above, what do you think Jesus meant by this?**

Jesus prophesied that the temple building would be destroyed (Luke 21:5-6), and, in fact, that very temple was destroyed by Roman forces in AD 70. But that temple was just a symbol, a way to remember that God intended to dwell with man.

But Jesus? Jesus is the true temple. Jesus is Emmanuel, God with us. And this temple, too, was destroyed, but then raised up in three days as Jesus prophesied. The true temple allowed no sin or even a "good" thing to get in the way of His love for the Father—yet His death and resurrection made atonement for the sin of others. Anyone who cries out "Hosanna! Save me!" to Him gains true connection to the Father through Jesus. And the furniture rearranging begins.

In a world that consistently values self-actualization, it can be understandably difficult for us to allow Jesus to be Lord of our lives—to have true authority over us and to "rearrange the furniture" as He sees fit. But the call for Jesus to save us is both a one-time call for salvation and an ongoing call for sanctification (the process of growing in godliness). Even after we are saved and belong to Him, sin is the enemy of home, so we have to trust God whenever He wants to rearrange the furniture. Although it may feel painfully countercultural, you can trust that He is the way home. Every sanctifying shift Jesus makes will make your heart a "homier" place for genuine worship and connection with Him.

Is Jesus making a sanctifying shift in your life right now? If so, describe the experience.

How can you encourage a friend who is working through a "furniture rearranging" moment?

DAY THREE

Jesus and Glory

If I was going to sum up the feeling of home in a preposition, first of all, I would be a nerd. Second of all, I am fine with being a nerd, and I would choose the word *with*. (If you remember, we considered this word a bit in Session 3. I guess I really do play favorites with the prepositions.)

I'd go so far as to say that the aim of God's story of home is *with*—God dwelling with man. So, since this study traces God's promise of home through Scripture, let's take a look at "God with us" throughout the story. (That's a pretty crucial aspect of home, isn't it?) After the sacred with-ness was severed in the garden, God provided other ways of with-ness, coming near to dwell with sinful people. Today we'll examine "God with us" by looking at the tabernacle, the temple, the exile and how they all point to Jesus, who is Immanuel, God with us.

TABERNACLE

LOOK UP EXODUS 40:34–38.

What covered the tabernacle?

What happened to Moses?

According to this text, did the Israelites know the way to the promised land?

In the wilderness, God's glory filled the tabernacle (v. 34), then settled—or dwelled—there (v. 35). The Israelites based their migration to the promised land on the movement of God. When He moved, they moved. This was the case "throughout all the stages of their journey" (v. 36). Wherever they went, God was with them.

TEMPLE

LOOK UP 1 KINGS 8:10-13.

What covered the temple?

What happened to the priests?

According to Solomon, how long would God dwell with them in this way?

In the promised land, God's glory filled the temple (v. 11), then settled—or dwelled—there (v. 13). The people of God were home, and God was with them. The tabernacle had pointed ahead to this.

Solomon's words about God dwelling in total darkness (v. 12) can be confusing because we usually associate glory with light. But surprisingly, God's glory is described as darkness in other passages. (In fact, Exodus 20:21 says, "And the people remained standing at a distance as Moses approached the total darkness where God was.") Solomon was likely quoting his father, David, who wrote "Clouds and total darkness surround him" in Psalm 97, a psalm all about God's glory. Perhaps the darkness was actually a kindness to people, who would die if they saw God directly—similar to the situation where God tucked Moses into the cleft of a rock in order to show Moses His glory in Exodus 33–34. For the sake of with-ness, God provides sinners with a covering.

EXILE

Remember the vision in Ezekiel 10? During exile, Ezekiel had a vision of God's presence leaving the temple. This moment was a gut punch—the total severing of home as they knew it. God was still I AM, but He removed the special expression of His presence from the sacred place. The temple was designed to be a glorious place where heaven and earth overlap, where God could dwell with man as He intended from the beginning, but God's people had "exchanged their Glory for useless idols" (Jer. 2:11b).

To have true home, to have glorious with-ness, God needed to provide a temple that could not be defiled.

JESUS

LOOK UP MATTHEW 3:13-17. **What in this text reminds you of the other texts we've read today?**

Similar to God's glory coming to rest on and dwell in the tabernacle and the temple, God's Spirit came to rest on Jesus! This happened at the very beginning of Jesus's ministry, and was essentially the dedication of the new and true temple. The whoosh in 1 Kings 8 pointed to this.

LOOK UP MATTHEW 17:1-6. **What in this text reminds you of the other texts we've read today?**

This passage describes an event we call "the transfiguration." The name may remind you of that butterfly word, *transformation*—Jesus was transformed before them. He was still Himself, but perhaps He was more Himself than they'd ever realized. It was as if Jesus's God-ness was suddenly unveiled to them. When God the Father spoke, perhaps this cloud was a lot like the one that covered the tabernacle and the temple!

LOOK UP MATTHEW 27:45-51. **How was this both a dark and a glorious moment?**

This scene of separation made the way for togetherness. As you may remember from our personal study in Session 3, the "curtain of the sanctuary" (v. 51) refers to the veil at the entrance of the holy of holies (the place where God's presence was said to abide). It separated the rest of the temple from this holy place. The high priest could pass through this veil only once a year, on the Day of Atonement (Ex. 26:33-35; Lev. 16:2). As I mentioned earlier in this study, a favorite kid's book of mine describes the veil as a "big KEEP OUT sign."⁹ But because of the sacrificial death of Jesus, the true temple, this barrier was gone. Christ made a way. He gave all of us access to God. The "keep out" sign became an invitation: "Come home."

LOOK UP JOHN 17:24 **and write it below.**

What did Jesus request and why?

God's glory is the ultimate welcome mat. It's pulling into the driveway and seeing the lights are on. It's everything that makes home *home*. God's glory can be seen through Jesus! And get this: Jesus promised that even after He ascended to heaven, He wouldn't leave His followers alone. God would still be with them in an even closer way than before. Jesus would send God the Spirit to live in His followers (John 14:16-17)!

Yes, there will certainly be times when we feel alone. But here's something truer than that feeling: God is with us.

DAY FOUR

Preparing a Place

Pre-motherhood, I thought pregnant people were being dramatic about the nesting thing. But the day I found myself hauling an 8x10 rug out of the nursery by myself at thirty-nine weeks pregnant, I had to take a hard look in the mirror. Inexplicably and suddenly, my brain insisted, "Rug is disgusting! I forbid Rug to be in the presence of Baby!" Then, to the dismay and alarm of Husband, I wielded my surprising pregnant lady strength to haul Rug downstairs. (Upon reflection, I think we put the rug back, and the baby was fine with it.) I was so deeply compelled to PREPARE A PLACE FOR THIS BABY, it was as if I'd been bitten by a radioactive spider.

Every time I've anticipated a child (both through pregnancy and through adoption), my internal affection for the child longs to express itself through my physical surroundings. You're probably familiar with what I'm talking about, whether through motherhood, preparing for a houseguest, or creating a shared space with roommates.

Perhaps you've also been the recipient of such affection—entering a place where it was clear you were prepared for, that your presence was anticipated with great joy.

If so, how did that impact your relationship with the preparer? What did the preparations mean to you?

If not, do you long for an experience like this? Explain, if possible.

Sometimes we're tempted to dismiss such preparations as superficial or silly—and of course, it could become either of those things, but at the core, "preparing a place" is image-bearer stuff. We saw this on display in Genesis 1–2 (think, for example, about how

God filled Eden with every tree with fruit that was good to eat and beautiful to look at!), and we learn this from Jesus Himself.

READ JOHN 14:1-7.

Jesus spoke these comforting words to His disciples the night before His violent departure from them. The beautiful togetherness Jesus's disciples enjoyed with Him was about to be severed—first through betrayal, then through abandonment, then through ridicule and torment, and finally through death on a cross. Jesus bore the full experience of separation, but His disciples experienced a measure of it, too.

What promises did Jesus offer to keep the hearts of the disciples from being troubled?

Thomas said he didn't know the way, but he knew the Way. In your own words, describe the difference.

How might Jesus's promises and proclamation (v. 6) have encouraged His disciples during His death and even after His ascension?

How do they encourage you today?

The cross was the ultimate act of hospitality. Jesus's death defeated the enemy of sin and made the way for anyone who looked to Him to be welcomed home. However, as we study God's promises of home, I don't want to deceive you into thinking that everyone who follows Jesus experiences a perfect home here and now. When we follow Jesus, our feet are placed solidly and permanently on the journey home. We also experience a "deposit" of true home through the indwelling of the Holy Spirit. (More on this in the next session.) But we're not fully home yet. As such, we experience a measure of separation that can be deeply painful, in a number of ways. And so, like Jesus's disciples, we find comfort and strength in Jesus's promises of home.

Let's press John 14:1-7 into the fabric of our own experiences.

Consider your current circumstances. You may not know the way—but you know the Way. Why is this a crucial comfort for the confusing zigs and zags of life? How does this encourage you right now?

Consider your anxieties about the future. How does knowing Jesus is (1) preparing a place for you and (2) will return for you make a difference on your journey?

All Christ followers experience "homesick" moments as we await Jesus's return. After all, we know home is where I AM is, and we long to be with Him fully in a place where the enemy cannot enter and where with-ness can flourish.

When do you most feel spiritually homesick? Why?

Let me offer you a bit of wording that has been a comfort to me during my "homesick" moments—those moments when I feel lonely, confused, overwhelmed, or exhausted by the impact of sin in my life and on the world. It's two phrases: "Christ in" and "in Christ."

CHRIST IN

LOOK UP THESE VERSES: ROMANS 8:10; 2 CORINTHIANS 13:5; GALATIANS 2:20.

Based on these verses, what do you think "Christ in" means?

How is the reality of Christ in you a "deposit of home" that can help you remember your true home in homesick moments?

IN CHRIST

LOOK UP THESE VERSES: ROMANS 8:1; 2 CORINTHIANS 5:17; GALATIANS 3:26.

Based on these verses, what do you think "in Christ" means?

How is the reality of being in Christ a "deposit of home" that can help you remember your true home in homesick moments?

Sister, if you are a Jesus follower, Christ is in you and you are in Christ. Christ dwells in you through God the Spirit. He is with you always. You are never alone, never forsaken. Moreover, because you are in Christ, when God looks at you, He sees Jesus. That means He looks at you as His true child. You are never unloved, never despised, never unwanted. You always belong.

"Christ in," and "in Christ": May these truths wrap around you like a blanket and warm you from within like a cup of coffee! It's all true: A precious deposit of home belongs to you, your true home is being prepared with you in mind, and Jesus will return so that you can be with Him. Thank you, God!

DAY FIVE

Where Are You?

Hebrews 2:17-18 tells us Jesus "had to be like his brothers and sisters in every way, so that he could become a merciful and faithful high priest in matters pertaining to God, to make atonement for the sins of the people. For since he himself has suffered when he was tempted, he is able to help those who are tempted."

It's a big deal that Jesus came to live as a human, like you, and to endure the pains of human life, like you. Jesus's ministry is deeply personal to us.

- He conquered sin—the enemy that threatens our homes.

- He understands the pain, loneliness, betrayal, and temptations we experience.

- He made the way home for us.

- He comforts us in our pain and helps us through difficult times.

- He helps us battle temptation and overcome sin.

Sister, you are seen, understood, fought for, and invited.

I want to share with you a letter from a fellow sister in Christ. As she shares her story of home, I hope it'll point you to God's story of home and give you an opportunity to notice where you are. May Jesus minister to you in that very place.

Dear Friend,

Have you ever experienced a deep longing for such a lengthy time that it feels like an old friend? The desire to belong has been that for me. I've dealt with it for a good while, but most acutely since getting married and moving to the United States.

You see, I am a half-Palestinian Dominican who became an American citizen through marriage and am now serving Christ in the Middle East. For most of my life I'd taken for granted what it felt like to belong. "Better together" had been a way of life for my community in the Dominican Republic. But on my wedding day I tearfully hugged my people goodbye and moved to a new city in the States.

My husband and I loved opening our home for hospitality. But at first, I couldn't quite tell who wanted us to be their people (mostly because I misread cultural cues). Just as I felt like it was starting to happen, we moved to a very international city in the Middle East. I didn't realize though that I had unresolved grief and patterns of seeking refuge in people as a way of coping with it.

Our time in that city would be relatively short due to my husband's work, so I jumped into trying to do life with God's people there. But many factors made doing life in community very challenging and my longing to belong was not met in church relationships the way I hoped. This revealed sinful patterns I had developed.

When the time came to say goodbye, the Lord pierced my soul through His Word:

"I, I am he who comforts you;
who are you that you are afraid of man who dies . . . ,
I am the LORD your God . . . [who says] to Zion, 'You are my people'"
(Isa. 51:12–16, ESV).

When I read the phrase, "You are my people," I burst out crying. I had been longing for years to hear other people say: "You guys are our people." But now here was the eternal God, establishing Himself as my place of belonging, and telling me, "Aylin, you are my people!"

Being in Christ reassures me that the things that matter to me, matter deeply to God because He is my Father. He sees my desert spaces and comforts me. He makes my wilderness flourish like Eden (Isa. 51:3). His delight in being close to His people never stops. He even rides the heavens to come near and rescue (Deut. 33:26)! He loves knowing us, hearing from us, and talking with us. The Spirit shines His light where we struggle to believe because He wants us to be filled with the hope of knowing His intimate love (Rom. 5:2). Sister, do you see how the Triune God is our tribe as we go through the changes of life?

continued →

I have moved cross-culturally twice more since that day the Lord spoke to me. With each move, my Father keeps peeling back the layers of my story, sinking in more deeply what it means to know Him as home. I am sure He is doing the same with you, my friend. I am thankful He doesn't stop preparing us this side of eternity for our life together with Christ, our bridegroom. "Til then, may His grace enable us to hear Him sing, "You are Mine, and I am yours."

— AYLIN MERCK, *writer, Middle East*

Use the space below (or your own journal) to respond to this letter. You may want to use the following questions to guide your response.

What thoughts and feelings are you experiencing as you consider this sister's story?

What from her letter most resonates with you and why?

How does her story help you understand God's story of home, reveal where you are, or help you find your way home to Him?

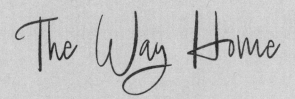

The Way Home

At the darkest moment
In the fullness of time
God sent the Way
To redeem all mankind

God came as a child
God came with a cry
God came without home
God came to die

He was the promised seed
Who came under Eden's sword
He was the true tabernacle
The God-with-us Lord

He was the true Temple
Upon Him was glory
The Way Home
Hope for exile's story

He lived the perfect life
The good news He proclaimed
Following the Father's will,
He took on our shame

He faced our great enemy
The sin that intruded
Into every human heart
Could now be uprooted

His tomb seemed the end
Sealed with a stone
But it could not hold Him
It wasn't His Home

We, the cursed,
Through Him are blessed
Our shame is gone
In His righteousness dressed

The darkness of sin
Has been overcome
By Jesus, the light
Who says to us, "Come!"

almost

home

session six

In him you are also being built together
for God's dwelling in the Spirit.

PAUL, EPHESIANS 2:22

Look, God's dwelling is with humanity,
and he will live with them.

A LOUD VOICE FROM THE THRONE,
REVELATION 21:3

Jesus didn't just fulfill promises; He made them. Before He returned to
heaven, Jesus promised He would send a Helper (the Holy Spirit), and He
promised He would return. These two promises are like fuel the rest of the
Bible runs on—and fuel that allows Christians ever since the time of Jesus
(including us!) to keep going. God Himself dwells in us, making us the
new temple. Because of Jesus, we have access to God no matter where we
are, no matter when we call, and no matter what we need. And though we
still endure the challenges of a world saturated with sin, we look ahead to
the day Jesus will return and finally make everything new and wonderful
forever. Sister, we are almost home.

VIEWER GUIDE
session six

Watch the Session Six video. Use this page to take notes, capture quotes, or doodle some thoughts from the video teaching session.

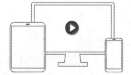

To access the video teaching sessions, use the instructions in the back of your Bible study book.

DISCUSSION/REFLECTION QUESTIONS

If you're doing this study with a group, be ready to discuss these questions during your time together. (If you're leading a group, check out the leader guide at lifeway.com/comehome to help you prepare.) If you're doing this study solo, use the following questions to reflect on what you've heard in the video teaching.

1 What is one thing in the video teaching that stood out to you? Why?

2 Do you ever spiritually get the feeling of not quite being home yet? If so, explain.

3 Is it a little strange to think about the Holy Spirit living inside you? How would you explain what that means to a child or a brand new Christian?

4 How has the Holy Spirit been a helper to you in the past few days and weeks?

5 How does Jesus's promise to bring you home impact the way you think, speak, and act in your current home?

6 As God's people, we are the "go and tell" temple. What does that mean and does that describe your church?

7 What are you currently doing to keep both the individual temple and the collective temple healthy and functioning for God's purpose and His glory?

8 If someone asked you what you learned in our time together today, what would you say?

DAY ONE

God's Posture Toward Those Who Come Home

The word *home* evokes feelings of deep comfort, intimacy, and belonging. So, sometimes when we speak about God's story of home, His invitation to us to "come home," and the new home where we will be with Him, there's a dissonance. After all, God is holy and perfect—how could sinners like us ever actually be home with Him? How can a holy God be comfortable with people like us? And how can people like us be comfortable with a holy God? Won't we feel unwanted on some level? Won't we suspect that He's a little grossed out by our sinfulness? Won't He be disappointed in us?

Even if you're a seasoned Christian, I suspect some part of this resonates with you or at least with someone you know.

Here's the tension for the Christian: We are not home yet, BUT we have been given a down payment of home. We often feel far away from God, BUT we walk in the double-layered promise of "in Christ" and "Christ in." We battle against our sin, BUT we know Jesus has conquered it.

In this tension, an accusation rises in our souls: God does not really want to be with us. Often the hardest thing to accept is the truth kids find so easy to sing: *Jesus loves me, this I know.* Do we?

Does this tension feel familiar to you? Explain.

Yes, the promises sound good. But are we truly loved by the Promise Keeper? Is God someone who does "good stuff" or is God good? And if God is good, will God be good to *me*?

We can all imagine what it's like to live with someone who is nice to you but would prefer that you aren't there. Maybe we're afraid God is like that. After all, He alone knows how we really are.

I recently confessed in my journal that I am "selfish, but in a spiritually clever way." Ouch. The "spiritually clever" is what God alone knows. I know how to trick you—and myself—into thinking I'm a good girl while secretly harboring pride and envy and contempt. I know God knows this too, so I'm sometimes suspicious of Him. Does He actually want me? Does He actually want to live with me? Does He actually love me and like me? It can feel hard to imagine.

This is why the promises of home are so very powerful—because they run deeper than God doing a thing. They are about God offering His very self.

READ LUKE 15:11-32.

THE YOUNGER SON (VERSES 11-20a)

How did the younger son treat his father?

What foolish choices did the younger son make and what were the consequences of those choices?

Verses 15-16 tells us the young man ended up tending pigs, longing to eat pig food because no one would give him anything. Seeing as how Jews consider pigs unclean animals, this was about as low as a Jewish person could go! But verse 17 is a huge turning point in the story. It says about the young man, "When he came to his senses" (CSB) or "But when he came to himself" (ESV).

What do you think this phrase means? Have you ever experienced something similar to this? Explain.

What resulted from the young man coming to his senses? What was his plan? What does this tell you about his heart?

What are the first few words of verse 20, and why are they critical to the younger son's story?

THE FATHER (VERSES 20b-24)

Normally, how would you expect a father who has been treated this way to respond to his son? How would you expect him to look (facial expression, posture, etc.)?

What does verse 20 tell you about the heart of the father toward his younger son?

It seems evident in verses 21-24 that the son's perceived "unworthiness" did not matter to the father. He did not relegate the son to a servant role; instead, He honored him and reestablished the younger son as part of the family.

What mattered most to the father, and how did he express his sentiment?

The father's love defies our imagination: a son deserving shame dared to hope for dutiful acceptance as a servant but was received with joyful celebration as a son!

THE OLDER SON (VERSES 25-32)

It's interesting that Jesus did not end the parable with the return of the son and the celebration that followed. He included another character in the story—the older son.

What was the older son's beef with his father? How does that resonate with you?

How does the older son's response reveal how scandalous the father's love is and that the older son is missing the point?

How do you relate to this story?

How do you see the heart of God in this parable?

Revelation 22:14 talks about those who've washed their robes and therefore can enter God's home and live with Him forever. And Revelation 7:14 tells us how robes are washed and made white: "They washed their robes and made them white in the blood of the Lamb." Those who have looked to Jesus in repentance and come to Him, no matter what pigsty they've been sitting in, are dressed gloriously and warmly welcomed to this new home.

In Dane Ortlund's massively influential book *Gentle and Lowly*, he shows how the Bible reveals Christ's very nature is to go toward sinners, toward the unclean, toward the ones that anyone else would look at and say "ick!" He says, "It is impossible for the affectionate heart of Christ to be overcelebrated, made too much of, exaggerated."[1]

Christ's heart for sinners is clear on the pages of Scripture. Why does it sometimes get so muddled in our hearts? Why, at times, do we understand it intellectually but not personally?

Despite our heads knowing God is good, our hearts sometimes won't dare to believe that He is good to us. Perhaps we lose sight of God's goodness when we are distracted by the world, by our stuff, by our own perceived "goodness," by the shame of our own sinfulness, by our social status, by our circumstances. When our attention from Him is diverted, our trust in Him deteriorates. We are unable to see Him as He actually is, and it gives the enemy an opportunity to whisper doubt in our ears. Whatever the case, too often I find myself hungry to know that He would actually run toward me, embrace me, and welcome me home!

God's love is not merely theological; it's personal. His promises of home are not merely intellectually ours; they're intimately ours. When the loud voice cries out from the throne in Revelation 21:3-4, it is a collective word for God's people, but it has an individual application for each of God's children!

> [3] Then I heard a loud voice from the throne: Look, God's dwelling is with humanity, and he will live with them. They will be his peoples, and God himself will be with them and will be their God. [4] He will wipe away every tear from their eyes. Death will be no more; grief, crying, and pain will be no more, because the previous things have passed away.

Sister, you specifically are loved and welcomed by God. His invitation to "come home" has your very name inscribed on it. He does not invite you for the sake of looking like a good God helping out a poor girl with nowhere to go. The invitation is the natural and beautiful extension of His goodness toward you, His longing to be with you, and His delight in you. Why? Because He loves you. Because through Christ, you are His. And so, He runs toward you with arms wide open.

Use the space below to process and ponder God's love for you. Confess what is hard for you to believe. Rejoice in what is true.

DAY TWO

Living Like We're Headed Home

When Peter preached that epic sermon at Pentecost (Acts 2:14-36), the listeners were "pierced to the heart" (Acts 2:37), meaning the Holy Spirit was convicting them of their need for God. They immediately asked Peter what they should do. His response: repent (which is what the prodigal son did when he "came to himself," realized his need, and went to the father), be baptized, and they would receive the gift of the Holy Spirit.

Peter described the Holy Spirit as a promise for all of God's children! He said, "For the promise is for you and for your children, and for all who are far off, as many as the Lord our God will call" (Acts 2:39). The moment anyone places faith in Jesus, that person is rescued from his or her sin and born into a forever family by the indwelling of the Holy Spirit.

> *Side note: Sometimes this passage is used to "prove" that baptism is required for salvation, or at least to receive the Holy Spirit. But we must always keep genre in mind when we're interpreting God's Word! Acts is historical narrative, not instruction. Peter's response offered an answer for exactly what the people asked—what they should do next—and was not intended to teach what is required for salvation or to receive the Holy Spirit.*

READ EZEKIEL 36:24-28.

What is God promising in this passage?

How is this fulfilled through the gift of the Holy Spirit?

How will this promise be fully, finally, and forever accomplished when Jesus returns?

God is transforming individuals who can and will follow Him fully and can therefore be totally at home with Him! Furthermore, God is building a family and a family home with people who are unified by their relationship to Him. Those of us who share DNA, addresses, languages, and customs can't begin to pull off the kind of unity that God is creating. This family is a miracle!

Of course, it's a miracle in process. In a way, the gift of the Holy Spirit is God's saying, "You are mine! Now, let me parent you." He is raising us up to look like Christ (Rom. 8:29) and to love one another—something we'll be able to do fully, finally, and forever when Jesus returns. We call this process sanctification.

But for now, it's not always pretty. Kids fall down when they're learning to walk, stumble over words when they're learning to talk, and make terrible judgment calls like running into the street, stealing a toy from a sibling, or eating ancient French fries from deep within the bowels of the car seat even though said fries are probably from the Mesozoic era. Being a kid can be messy—so can being God's kid. If you've spent any time in a relationship with another Christian or ever entered the inner-world of a church environment, you know what I mean. Perhaps you've found yourself ironically enraged that you're not patient yet, snipped at your kids while you're reading your Bible, or experienced road rage while the Christian radio station plays in the background. If so, you get it.

It's all a reminder that we desperately need God, that salvation is an immediate thing but also an ongoing thing. We're not home yet. The New Testament letters are clear that we are called to ongoing participation in the parenting God offers, which Paul was talking about in Ephesians when he said we are to be "growing into maturity" and are to "grow in every way into (Christ)" (Eph. 4:13,15). Paul cautioned the Ephesians to be careful how they walk (Eph. 5:15), saying they (and we!) should "be imitators of God, as dearly loved children, and walk in love" (Eph. 5:1-2a) and "walk as children of light" (Eph. 5:8).

The call to "walk as children of light" and live by the Spirit is both an individual call and a collective call. It's a way we "rehearse" our true family and our true home and the way we experience closeness with the Lord while we await Jesus's return. It's challenging and yet it is the life-giving way—because God's way is always life-giving.

Let's investigate what it looks like to rehearse our true home and true family.

READ 1 PETER 2:1-12.

Peter is writing to Christians he called "exiles" because they, like us, were awaiting Christ's return. Additionally, they were enduring persecution that likely made them feel like strangers in their own hometowns. During this time in history, widespread horrors were inflicted upon Christians by leaders like Nero, Domitian, and Trajan.[2] Peter was concerned for how they were living out their faith in the midst of all this terror. Though the gospel teaches us that we can't earn our way into God's favor by the way we live, the way Christians live impacts our fellowship with the Lord and how clearly others hear God's invitation to "come home."

What should we as Christians get rid of, and what should we desire?

How was Peter challenging believers with the illustration of a newborn's desire for milk (v. 2)?

Peter was calling us to long for the nutritious Word of God. It's through the goodness of God's Word that we will grow up into Him. He referenced Psalm 34:8, which says, "Taste and see that the LORD is good." When we have experienced God's goodness, we will want more. And continuing to taste of His goodness through relationship with Him, we will grow!

How have you experienced the goodness of God's Word?

What might numb your spiritual taste buds?

REVIEW 1 PETER 2:4-10. **Note below how Jesus is described and how believers are described in these verses.**

JESUS	BELIEVERS
v. 4	v. 5
vv. 6-8	v. 9
	v. 10

How is our purpose described in this passage?

Verse 5

Verse 9

How is sin described in verse 11, and why should believers not live a sinful lifestyle?

Peter was counseling these believers to honor their true home by not letting sin make its home in their hearts.

In what areas of your life are you tempted to let sin make its home in your heart?

How do the truths found in 1 Peter 2:1-12 help you in your battle against sin?

Have you ever been worried about something, sought counsel from a friend about your concern, and her advice was, "Don't worry about it"? My internal response in those situations is always, "OH! WHAT A GREAT IDEA! IT NEVER OCCURRED TO ME TO JUST NOT WORRY ABOUT WHAT I'M WORRIED ABOUT!" In the same way, when we receive counsel not to sin, we automatically know it's not as simple as just not doing it. That's why Peter attempted to set believers' sights on (1) who Jesus is, (2) who we are because of Jesus, and (3) our hope ahead. His words also urge us to examine our lives to know what to put away, to remember God's goodness, and to long for the proper things.

What helps you remember these three things?

One day, our character will perfectly mirror Christ's, and our family will be unified in a way that proclaims God's goodness and power. Until then, we commit to the slow growth made possible by our active participation with the Holy Spirit.

Based on today's texts, why is it important for Christians to live in a way that honors God?

How do we continue to walk faithfully when we've failed, we're exhausted, or life is just hard?

DAY THREE
Entering into God's Rest

When my daughter was three, we had to move away from the only home she'd known—and she suddenly stopped sleeping. She'd always been this impressive snoozer, clocking a solid twelve hours every night and topping it off with a three-hour nap each day. To protect any moms of toddlers reading this from having to contend with their envy, please know that when she turned two and a half, she dropped the naps cold turkey. This was right around the time her baby brother started crawling and eating anything he found on the floor, including one old spider that haunts my dreams. (I can still see him delightedly gumming that dead spider, knowing I wouldn't get to him in time before he ingested it. Protein?) The nap-quitting did a number on my sanity (as did the spider-eating), but when our move impacted the sacred twelve hours each night, I was beside myself.

Every night, she'd cry, "I want to go to the house with the yellow door!" Baby girl was homesick. She couldn't rest because she longed to be at the place where she felt at home.

Do you ever struggle to rest when you're not at home? If so, why do you think that is?

Now, never say this to a mom enduring the perils of sleepless children, but not being able to sleep away from home is actually a very biblical response.

God created the earth in a set of seven days, which culminated in His rest. In doing so, He set a pattern of sevens and-entering-into-rest that we see throughout Scripture that points to our true home.

LET'S LOOK AT HEBREWS 4:1-11.

The CSB translation calls this section of Hebrews 4 "The Promised Rest." In the verses leading up to this chapter, the author of Hebrews discussed how Moses, God's servant, was supposed to lead the Israelites into God's "rest" in the promised land, but because of their unbelief, they were not able to enter (Heb. 3:16-19). They allowed sin to make its home in their hearts, so God's promised land and rest were for the next generation. The author was using this part of the biblical story to help his readers understand their current spiritual position and the rest provided by Jesus they could step into if they remained faithful.

Read the text, and in your Bible, (circle) or note anything you find about rest.

> *By the way, the text includes some specific Old Testament quotes: verses 3 and 5: Psalm 95:11; verse 4: Genesis 2:2; verse 7: Psalm 95:7-8.*

What parts of the biblical story are mentioned here? *(It's always a good idea to pay attention when the Bible draws "arrows" to other parts of the story!)*

Are there any verses that confuse you? List them below or draw a question mark in the margin. *(Often when our attention spans drift, it's a sign that we feel confused and are mentally retreating. So pay attention to the drift, and you may realize there's a question at the core of it!) Paying attention to questions is helpful, but it's also helpful to do something with our questions! Sometime this week, share your questions with a friend, spouse, or pastor who may be able to help you process them. Or, you may find that you discover clarity for a past question in a future day of Bible reading! I love when this happens.)*

> *I learned this from my friend Toni Yglesias, who has taught the women at my church to study the Bible by using her expertise in critical thinking skills and methodology. Thanks, Toni!*

How did the Israelites of Moses's day "fall short" of entering into God's rest?

Joshua led the generation after Moses into the promised land, "God's rest." How did this rest fall short of the "Sabbath rest [that] remains for God's people" (vv. 8-9)?

How does the promised land point to the gospel? In other words, how is knowing God like one giant Sabbath?

While the people of God had political rest when they entered the promised land, they did not experience the rest that comes through the gospel—the rest experienced through the cleansing of their sins. That rest is only found through faith in Christ. This gospel rest is a deposit of the true rest to come in our true home. (This is similar to how the indwelling of the Holy Spirit is a "deposit" of our true home and the togetherness we'll experience there.)

Would you say your life is shaped around hustle (what you do) or rest (knowing what God has done)? A bit of both? Explain.

What do you think a gospel-honoring, Sabbath-shaped life might look like?

Do you long for a deeper experience of rest? If so, try to put words to this longing.

Interestingly, the Bible talks about an ultimate Sabbath—which points us to the true rest to come. If you've ever read the Old Testament and found reference to "the year of Jubilee," you've read about the Sabbath-est Sabbath. (My term. I know it's terrible.)

READ LEVITICUS 25:8-22.

The year of Jubilee was a once-in-a-lifetime experience for God's people. Since it happened every "seven sevens" (forty-nine years), every person would be able to experience it once—maybe twice.

How would the land get to "rest" during this year?

How would people's daily lives and relationships be different during this year?

Based on their continual disregard for God's Word in the years leading up to the exile, we can suspect that God's people were not faithful to "enter in" to this rest every forty-nine years (Jer. 25:2-7)[3]. (In fact, since there aren't any narratives at all in Scripture of God's people observing the year of Jubilee, some have suggested that it was never once observed!)

Interestingly, in 1 and 2 Chronicles (an overview of Israel's history that was collected during and after the exile), the Chronicler framed up the exile within the idea of rest. He said that God "deported those who escaped from the sword to Babylon . . . and the land enjoyed its Sabbath rest all the days of the desolation until seventy years were fulfilled" (2 Chron. 36:20-21). It's as if the land finally got all those years of Jubilee that it had been denied.[4]

It's ironic that the land experienced God's promise of rest while God's people were away from home. But someday, all of it will come together. The people and the place will enter into God's rest—and like the Day of Atonement, it'll begin with the sound of a trumpet.

Look up the following verses. What do they all say will happen?

Matthew 24:29-31

1 Corinthians 15:51-52

1 Thessalonians 4:16-18

Revelation 11:15

When my daughter stopped sleeping, the only thing I could find to help her rest in our "in-between" home was—are you ready for this—a horrifically tacky set of *Trolls*-themed sheets. (This continues to make no sense to me. But colorful sheets delighted her, and she slept.) But eventually, we settled into a new home, and that's when she truly began to rest again. She loves our home now even more than the house with the yellow door.

At the risk of overworking this metaphor, Jesus's followers have entered into God's rest like a little girl with *Trolls* sheets. The gospel is a delight, a rescue, and an invitation to rest even when we feel we're in exile. Praise God! But something more lies ahead. Jesus will return to usher us into the homiest home, and when that happens, we will enter into the true rest for which our exhausted souls so deeply long.

DAY FOUR

When Heaven Comes Home

In high school, I remember a classmate saying with a laugh, "I want to go to hell because that's where my friends will be." It was a spicy, unserious response to God that was designed to make us nearby Christians squirm a bit. As I look back, I realize his statement also revealed a short-sighted, yet popular view of heaven—heaven is the place where goody-goody people go to play a harp while sitting on a cloud. If that's the case, then yeah, hell seems like a more exciting place where it just so happens the air conditioning went out.

Obviously, this classmate didn't have a very biblical view of heaven, but I honestly didn't either! At that time, I saw heaven as a place where everyone acts right and wears white. Probably many Christians have a faulty view of heaven. It's understandable in some ways. The clear information on our forever home is limited. However, one of the main promises of heaven we can cling to is that we will be with God (2 Cor. 5:8). At this point in this study, you are probably beginning to grasp that this truth is the deep craving of our souls—even for my classmate, who clearly longed for the friendship, joy, and fun that can be found in God alone. But one of the other main promises of heaven is something that hasn't happened in fullness yet—that God will be with us on earth. The new earth.

Randy Alcorn says, "When God's children die, we immediately go to heaven to be with Christ (Luke 23:43). But when we carefully read Scripture, we find that one day God will permanently relocate the present heaven to the newly transformed earth, which then will become the 'forever heaven.'"[5]

This is why the last three chapters of the Bible are so fascinating—especially when we view them in light of the first three chapters of the Bible. We are able to gather so many details about the forever home, about the place that Nancy Guthrie says is "even better than Eden."[6] Since we know how awesome Eden was, this is a bold and exciting claim!

Let's look at the "even better than Eden" home that awaits us by comparing the beginning with the end. Like the most epic of home-makeover shows, the Bible intentionally offers some incredible "before and afters."

Fill out the chart below by looking up the verses listed and describing the following elements. (This looks like a lot of flipping around, but you'll simply be going back and forth . . . excited to make some new connections. I did a couple to get you started. I did a couple to get you started.)

	EDEN (GEN. 1–2)	EDEN AFTER SIN (GEN. 3)	NEW HEAVEN AND EARTH (REV. 20–22)
TREE OF LIFE	2:9 It was beautiful to look at and good to eat.	3:22-24 It became off limits because of sin.	22:2 It will be flourishing, providing fruit and healing.
FEATURES OF THE LAND	2:8-14 God planted a beautiful garden to provide for them.	3:17-19 Ground was cursed, filled with thorns and hard to work.	22:1-3 No longer cursed. Fruitful and life-giving.
BRIDE/ BRIDEGROOM	2:18-25	3:12,16	21:2
SATAN AND SIN	3:1	3:14-15	20:10; 21:27
BLESSING/ CURSE	1:28	3:16-19	21:4; 22:3
DEATH	2:16-17	3:20-24	20:14; 21:4
TOGETHERNESS WITH GOD	1:28; 2:8; 3:8	3:8-10	21:3; 22:4

The new heaven and new earth will be such a far cry from "sitting on clouds with harps." It will be the culmination of every wonderful thing. And the core reason for being wonderful is not because of the features—but because of the Father. Think about it: We won't just hear His sound in the garden like Adam and Eve did (Gen. 3:8,10), we will see His face (Rev. 22:4).

Have you seen those videos of babies with impaired vision getting glasses that allow them to see for the first time? I once watched a compilation video of dozens of these events, and by the end, I was ugly-crying. It was so beautiful and moving to watch the delight on the babies' faces when they finally and fully saw their parents' faces, finally and fully recognized the ones whose love they'd experienced day in and day out. And my thought was, "Maybe it'll be like that when I see Jesus." On that day, we'll see Him, and we'll know we're home.

> **What part of the new heaven and new earth do you most anticipate? What feels like the biggest relief right now? Explain.**

In 1 Thessalonians 4:16-18, it says, "For the Lord himself will descend from heaven with a shout, with the archangel's voice, and with the trumpet of God, and the dead in Christ will rise first. Then we who are still alive, who are left, will be caught up together with them in the clouds to meet the Lord in the air, and *so we will always be with the Lord*. Therefore *encourage one another* with these words" (emphasis added).

We are to encourage one another with the promise of Jesus's return. The final chapters of the Bible help us understand why this is such an encouraging promise. Every longing of our hearts will be fulfilled; every horror of our lives will be redeemed. We will fully, finally, and forever be home—because we will be with God, and God will be with us.

How can the new heaven and new earth be an encouragement to someone you know? Consider this, and in the coming days, look for an opportunity to "give an answer to everyone who asks you to give the reason for the hope that you have" (1 Pet. 3:15, NIV).

As you know, this study is called *Come Home*. These words are our invitation, our evangelism, our hope and heart cry.

INVITATION

LOOK UP REVELATION 22:17. **What is the invitation to all people and who does the inviting? What does it cost to come?**

EVANGELISM

LOOK UP MATTHEW 28:18-20. **These are some of Jesus's last words before He ascended to heaven. They are a crucial commissioning for His followers as they await their true home. What is involved in our inviting people to "come"? What promise does Jesus offer as we do this inviting?**

OUR HOPE AND HEART CRY

LOOK UP REVELATION 22:20 **and write it below.**

This hope and heart cry holds an important place in Scripture as the second-to-the-last verse in the Bible. Ever since this letter of Revelation was first read by early Christians, Jesus followers have been clinging to this promise, and joining with John in this heart cry: "Come, Lord Jesus!"

Perhaps you've noticed that Christians often say this when something terrible happens in the world. We don't say it to be trite; we utter it because we believe God's promises and are clinging to them in faith. It's something we express when the world's horrors leave us wordless. This phrase offers the world our greatest hope: Jesus is coming.

What makes you long for Jesus's return?

How does the promise of our ultimate home affect how you walk out your story of home?

DAY FIVE

Where Are You?

When our stories of home are wonderful, we rejoice in the promise of true home. What we currently experience is a glimmer of something better!

When our stories of home are terrible, we cling to the promise of true home. Something better than what we've experienced is coming.

You may remember that Moses, a man who never really had a home, wrote in Psalm 90:1, "Lord, through all the generations you have been our home!" (NLT). Revelation 21:3 takes this true statement to the next level:

> I heard a loud shout from the throne, saying, "Look, God's home is now among his people! He will live with them, and they will be his people. God himself will be with them" (NLT).

Jesus is coming to make a new heaven and a new earth where we will fully, finally, and forever be with Him, safe from sin and death and enjoying true togetherness with our true family.

I want to share with you a letter from a fellow sister in Christ. As she shares her story of home, I hope it will point you to God's story of home and give you an opportunity to notice where you are. May Jesus minister to you in that very place.

Dear Friend,

It was December of my fourth-grade year. I ran home from school, elated because I had been cast in the lead role in my school Christmas play. I was finally getting a chance to be a part of something, to belong. See, that year had already been a bit of a roller coaster, and if I am honest all the years leading up to it were too. Our family had already moved four times that school year and about a dozen prior to that. I had not really had a chance to make friends or feel like a normal kid, but this play felt like a glimpse of normalcy. As I turned the corner onto our street my heart dropped. There was a moving truck in our driveway . . . again. I walked up on legs of stone, dreading what came next. Sure enough, we were moving. By the end of the weekend, we would be in a new home in a new state (the third one that year). By the end of that school year, we would be on our eighth move of the year and once again in a new state. I had completely stopped talking at school. I was so weary of trying to explain that—no we weren't military, no I wasn't a foster kid, no we weren't running from the law, and no I didn't think my parents were secretly spies. I just shut down and stopped trying to belong. In my experience, making friends just meant losing friends. A kid can only say so many goodbyes before you stop wanting to say hello.

Now in adulthood, I have lived in over fifty different places, houses, apartments, dorm rooms and even briefly in my car. In all these places, I have never felt at home. I have been a wanderer in the wilderness, desperately seeking my promised land, my home, my place where I belonged both physically and in community. I have dreamt of a porch with creaking rocking chairs leading to a home chock-full of memories and loved ones. A place my children's children will always know as a haven, rooted in love. Instead, my life has been filled with moving boxes that never quite get fully unpacked and suitcases at the ready, because this is just another temporary stop.

I have cried out to God with weary tears asking—when will I be home? I have been frustrated at myself for not having patience in God's timing. I have also sat in awe as I look back at my journey, praising God for the epic adventures He has brought me through. God has blessed me with a husband that grew up with a completely different story, who reminds me that I am home if I am with my family. I have seen firsthand how my journey has equipped me with a strong ability to adapt and lean into the unwavering truth of God and his faithfulness to be at my side through it all.

The lord has lovingly led me to his word in the story of Moses. Moses was called on to lead his people through the wilderness for years just trying to reach the promised land. As he journeyed, he struggled, he had moments of wavering faith, he was

continued →

weary, and he yearned to be home. But through this, he also experienced some epic moments. While Moses was kept from entering the promised land here on earth, he can rejoice in the eternal promised land. And in that same eternal promised land, is a place for me. I can rest in knowing that all homes under the sun are temporary. I see how God is growing me, preparing me, and encouraging me towards true connection. Even in my impatience, God is faithful and, in His timing, in His design, I will have a home.

— SALINA KELLEY, *Administrative Assistant at Lifeway Women, Tennessee*

Use the space below (or your own journal) to respond to this letter. You may want to use the following questions to guide your response.

What thoughts and feelings are you experiencing as you consider this sister's story?

What from her letter most resonates with you and why?

How does her story help you understand God's story of home, reveal where you are, or help you find your way home to Him?

Almost Home

To those His friends
Jesus promised two things
He would send a Helper,
And soon return as King

All the promises we've collected
Will be made manifest
We'll know it to be true
Every word that He said

So in faith we practice home
In faith we battle sin
That rises up between us
Especially what's within

It has no place among us
This temple where God lives
So as we walk by the Spirit
We repent, we forgive

When our steps get weary
We keep our gaze ahead
We wrap up in His promises
We cling to every thread

So sister, keep moving forward
You are almost home
With every shaking step
Know you're not alone

Soon He will return
To make all things right
No more tears or death
No more sin to fight

Every longing of your heart
Every piece of your story
Will all be made new
Will all become glory

Don't let your heart be troubled
Keep putting on the armor
It won't be long now
Home is just around the corner

the story
of home

session seven

We've looked at God's story for the past six weeks, but as part of our final time together, I want to tell you the whole story in one swoop. The aim today isn't to study it but to step into it. I'm hoping this brief, narrative overview will help you *experience* God's story, make new connections to it, and love God and His Word even more deeply. I suggest you and the women you're studying with consider this time a "closing ceremonies" of sorts, a way to sear the story into your consciences, a way to step into the story beyond your place as Bible student but as a recipient of the promises. This is, of course, God's story—but in His goodness He decided it ought to be yours, too. This is The Story of Home.

VIEWER GUIDE

session seven

Watch the Session Seven video. Use this page to take notes, capture quotes, or doodle some thoughts from the video teaching session.

To access the video teaching sessions, use the instructions in the back of your Bible study book.

DISCUSSION/REFLECTION QUESTIONS

If you're doing this study with a group, be ready to discuss these questions during your time together. (If you're leading a group, check out the leader guide at lifeway.com/comehome to help you prepare.) If you're doing this study solo, use the following questions to reflect on what you've heard in the video teaching.

1 What is one thing in the video teaching that stood out to you? Why?

2 How does hearing the story of home in Scripture told in one sitting help you better understand God's character and purpose?

3 What session of this study has been your favorite? Why?

4 What is one thing you've learned in your journey home that you'd love to pass on to someone younger in age or younger in the faith than you? Who's a person you can share that with?

5 What do you most look forward to in our forever home? Why?

6 If someone asked you what you learned in this Bible study what would you say?

7 How do you need to apply what you've learned from this study?

If I Could Build You a House

(A POEM FOR BAILEY)

If I could build a house
where pain couldn't root
where disease couldn't grow
where separation had no strength,
I would.
I would build it for you.

The roof would be firm in the storms
The walls would keep your body safe
The doors would say to pain,
"You are not welcome here."

In the garden, togetherness would grow
and it would not stop
It would cover the house like ivy
It would fill the space between us
like a fragrance
like the glow of a candle

We would pick the
togetherness like berries
We would serve it at our table
in big heaping bowls
We would store the extras in our cabinets
and it would spill out
everywhere. Everywhere.
With berry-stained hands,
we would laugh over the lovely mess
together. Together.

But togetherness doesn't grow like that,
not here.
Here we are apart.
Here my tools are faulty
Here my materials too weak
I would build it for you,
but I cannot.

Here tornados rip off roofs like a lid
Here doors can't keep out the pain and the hate
Here cancer grows where it was not planted
where it is not welcome
Here it takes what it was never given
And eats of the berries we so carefully collected
And smashes the space between us
This is not the house I would make for you.
If I could build another, I would
And yet, among these cracks and leaks
and these rusted hinges,
despite all the weak,
I notice something about our feet:
They are standing on something
strong.

I stomp and feel it firm beneath
Something built with hands not ours,
with tools not ours
Something built by Someone
who would build it
and could build it.

Someone who did not shut out pain
but welcomed it in,
who said to the winds and the disease
to the sin and the shame:
Come in my house instead.
Someone who surrendered his body
who gave up his home
who withheld not one cell
from the destruction we fear

And then from the ashy heap
he constructed this thing under
our feet
and despite all the shaking
it hasn't moved an inch.
Somehow in all the dying
the soil is still rich.
Somehow in all the separation
I can spot togetherness that grows
and cannot stop.

Darling, while much is lost
and much has been endured,
stomp and feel it firm beneath:
The foundation is unchanged.
No matter how our house shakes,
Nothing can stop this sprout of hope:
Of another home that our Builder is making

He is placing its foundation
In a place with no storms
Where you'll be perfectly safe
Where pain cannot come
because it does not know the way
A place with a garden where togetherness grows
and it cannot stop

It will cover the house like ivy
It will fill the space between us
like a fragrance
like the glow of a candle

In that house, one day,
we will pick the togetherness like berries
We will serve it at our table
in big heaping bowls

We will store the extras
in our cabinets
and it will spill out
everywhere. Everywhere.
With berry-stained hands,
we will laugh over the lovely mess
together. Together.

And our Builder will be there with us
(after all, it's his feast)
and we'll look at him in awe, saying,
"We can't believe you made this!
We can't believe you made space for us!"
He'll stretch out his hands,
stained with blood and with berries,
draw us in close
and never let go.
Not ever. Not ever.

Written in honor and memory of my friend and former student Bailey Purkey, who
passed away in 2020 of Small Cell Ovarian Cancer at twenty one years old.

Endnotes

Session One

1. Victor P. Hamilton, *The Book of Genesis, Chapters 1–17, The New International Commentary on the Old Testament* (Grand Rapids: Wm. B. Eerdmans Publishing Co., 1990), 192.

2. Nancy Guthrie, *Blessed*, (Wheaton: Crossway, 2022), p. 234.

3. Ādām: Strong's H120, Blue Letter Bible, accessed November 28, 2023, https://biblehub.com/hebrew/120.htm.

4. K. J. Ramsey, *This Too Shall Last* (Grand Rapids: Zondervan Reflective, 2020), 110.

Session Two

1. Moisés Silva and Merrill Chapin Tenney, The Zondervan Encyclopedia of the Bible, A-C (Grand Rapids, MI: The Zondervan Corporation, 2009), 17.

2. Shamar: Strong's H8104, Bible Hub, accessed November 28, 2023, https://biblehub.com/hebrew/8104.htm.

3. Malcom B. Yarnell III, Hebrews Study Note, *CSB Study Bible* (Nashville: Holman Bible Publishers, 2017), 1958.

4. Cambridge Advanced Learner's Dictionary & Thesaurus, (Cambridge: Cambridge University Press, 2013), s.v. "homebody," accessed November 28, 2023, https://dictionary.cambridge.org/us/dictionary/english/homebody.

5. Oxford Languages Dictionary, s.v. "better," accessed November 29, 2023, google.com.

6. Zera: Strong's H2233, Bible Hub, accessed November 29, 2023, https://biblehub.com/hebrew/2233.htm.

Session Three

1. M. Weinfeld, "kābôd" in *Theological Dictionary of the Old Testament*, ed. G. Johannes Botterweck, Helmer Ringgren, and Heinz-Josef Fabry, trans. David E. Green (Grand Rapids; Cambridge: William B. Eerdmans Publishing Company, 1995), 23.

2. Michael Reeves, "The Difference Jesus Makes: To Your View of God," Union Publishing, accessed November 29, 2023, https://www.uniontheology.org/resources/doctrine/god/the-difference-jesus-makes-1-to-your-view-of-god.

3. John Piper, "Can We See God or Not?" Desiring God, Episode 1005, February 20, 2017, https://www.desiringgod.org/interviews/can-we-ever-see-god-or-not.

4. Douglas K. Stuart, Exodus, vol. 2, *The New American Commentary* (Nashville: Broadman & Holman Publishers, 2006), 698.

5. "What Was the Tabernacle?" Thomas Nelson Bibles blog, Adapted from the King James Study Bible, Full Color Edition, May 18, 2022, https://www.thomasnelsonbibles.com/blog/what-was-the-tabernacle/.

6. Carl Laferton, *The Garden, the Curtain, and the Cross*, (UK: The Good Book Company, 2016).

7. Elizabeth Woodson, *Embrace Your Life* (Nashville: B & H Publishing Group, 2022), 109.

Session Four

1. D Ralph H. Alexander, "Ezekiel," in *The Expositor's Bible Commentary: Isaiah, Jeremiah, Lamentations, Ezekiel*, ed. Frank E. Gaebelein, vol. 6 (Grand Rapids: Zondervan Publishing House, 1986), 754.

2. David W. Stowe, Song of Exile: *The Enduring Mystery of Psalm 137* (New York: Oxford University Press, 2016), 9.

3. Yhvh: Strong's H3068, Bible Hub, accessed November 29, 2023, https://biblehub.com/hebrew/3068.htm.

4. Tim Keller, "Praying Our Anger," Gospel in Life, April 28, 2002, https://gospelinlife.com/downloads/praying-our-anger-5269/.

5. Paul Carter, "Dashing the Little Ones Against the Rock — Does this Verse Really Belong in Scripture," The Gospel Coalition, July 5, 2017, https://ca.thegospelcoalition.org/columns/ad-fontes/dashing-little-ones-rock-verse-really-belong-scripture/.

6. Sam Kneller, Biblical Hebrew— An Amazing Language, Both Simple and Deep at the Same Time, Medium, August 9, 2019, https://medium.com/the-explanation/biblical-hebrew-an-amazing-language-both-simple-and-deep-at-the-same-time-efdc8fa1ba3a.

7. Paul Carter, "Dashing the Little Ones Against the Rock — Does this Verse Really Belong in Scripture," The Gospel Coalition, July 5, 2017, https://ca.thegospelcoalition.org/columns/ad-fontes/dashing-little-ones-rock-verse-really-belong-scripture/. https://ca.thegospelcoalition.org/columns/ad-fontes/dashing-little-ones-rock-verse-really-belong-scripture/

8. Keller, "Praying Our Anger," Gospel in Life, April 28, 2002, https://gospelinlife.com/downloads/praying-our-anger-5269/.

9. David W. Stowe, Song of Exile: The Enduring Mystery of Psalm 137 (New York: Oxford University Press, 2016), 3.

10. John Collins and Tim Mackie, "The Significance of Seven," BibleProject Podcast, Episode 2, October 21, 2019, https://bibleproject.com/podcast/significance-7/.

11. David Guzik, "Daniel 9 — The Seventy Weeks of Daniel," Enduring Word, 2018, accessed November 29, 2023, https://enduringword.com/bible-commentary/daniel-9/.

Session Five

1. Sympatheō: Strong's G4834, Blue Letter Bible, accessed November 29, 2023, https://www.blueletterbible.org/lexicon/g4834/kjv/tr/0-1/.

2. Andreas J. Kostenberger and Alexander E. Stewart, The First Days of Jesus (Wheaton: Crossway, 2015), 140.

3. Ibid., 79.

4. Hosanna: Strong's H5614, accessed January 16, 2023, https://biblehub.com/greek/5614.htm.

5. Stuart K. Weber, Matthew, Holman New Testament Commentary, (Nashville: Broadman & Holman Publishers, 2000) Matthew 21:12.

6. Tim Keller, "The Cross and the Temple" Sermon, Gospel in Life, June 20, 2022, https://podcast.gospelinlife.com/e/the-cross-and-the-temple/.

7. Ibid.

8. "Temple," BibleProject, video, September 5, 2019, https://bibleproject.com/explore/video/temple/.

9. Carl Laferton, The Garden, the Curtain, and the Cross, (UK: The Good Book Company, 2016).

Session Six

1. Dane Ortland, Gentle and Lowly, (Wheaton: Crossway, 2020), 29.

2. "1 Peter," The Jesus Bible, (Grand Rapids: Zondervan, 2019), 1870.

3. Jon Collins and Tim Mackie, "Jubilee: The Radical Year of Release," BibleProject Podcast, Episode 8, November 25, 2019, https://bibleproject.com/podcast/jubilee-radical-year-release/.

4. John Collins and Tim Mackie, "Seventy Times Seven – Prophetic Math," BibleProject Podcast, Episode 10, December 9, 2019, https://bibleproject.com/podcast/seventy-times-seven-prophetic-math/.

5. Randy Alcorn, "Forever: Made for a Different Place," The Jesus Bible, (Grand Rapids: Zondervan, 2019), 1938.

6. Nancy Guthrie, Even Better Than Eden, (Wheaton: Crossway, 2018).

Get the most from your study.

Customize your Bible study time with a guided experience.

In this study you'll:

- Unpack the theme of home found throughout Scripture.

- Identify your spiritual homesickness and be equipped to process your longing for home through God's story.

- Understand how God's promise of a true, forever home is better than any home we have experienced.

- Find freedom from the pressure of maintaining the image of a perfect home.

To enrich your study experience, consider the accompanying video teaching sessions from Caroline Saunders, approximately 35–35 minutes each.

STUDYING ON YOUR OWN?

Watch Caroline Saunders' teaching sessions, available via redemption code for individual video-streaming access, printed in this Bible study book.

LEADING A GROUP?

Each group member will need a *Come Home* Bible study book, which includes video access. Because all participants will have access to the video content, you can choose to watch the videos outside of your group meeting if desired. Or, if you're watching together and someone misses a group meeting, they'll have the flexibility to catch up! A DVD set is also available to purchase separately if desired.

Browse study formats, a free session sample, video clips, church promotional materials, and more at

lifeway.com/comehome